TWO
TEMPLE PLACE

'A PERFECT GEM' OF LATE VICTORIAN ART, ARCHITECTURE AND DESIGN

BARBARA BRYANT

TWO
TEMPLE
PLACE

The Bulldog Trust

Two Temple Place is part of The Bulldog Trust, Registered Charity No. 1123081

Published in Great Britain in 2013
by Two Temple Place
2 Temple Place,
London WC2R 3BD
www.twotempleplace.org

Two Temple Place is part of The Bulldog Trust
Registered Charity No. 1123081

A catalogue record for this publication
is available from the British Library

ISBN 978-0-9570628-2-5

Designed and produced by NA Creative

Typeset in Perpetua

Printed in the UK

COVER
Weathervane ship on top of Two Temple Place

FRONTISPIECE
Decorated brackets under the oriel windows of Two Temple Place

PHOTOGRAPHIC CREDITS
All modern colour photographs of Two Temple Place are by Julian Nieman.
Figs 4 & 6 are by the author; figs 16, 21, 33, 83
(Centre for Buckinghamshire Studies, Aylesbury) by Peter Hoare,
figs 76–78 by Sean Thorpe and fig. 46 by Will Pryce.

PREFACE

WELCOME TO TWO TEMPLE PLACE, HOME OF THE BULLDOG TRUST

Two Temple Place was first built as a private residence for one of the world's wealthiest men, and we are delighted to share its beauty with the wider public.

The Bulldog Trust was founded in 1983, to act as a catalyst for charitable initiatives. Although a small organisation, with limited financial resources, we pride ourselves on our creativity and flexibility in designing our programmes, gifts and support to maximise the charity impact. Our donations are structured to unlock other resources, address funding gaps, transform organisations by providing assistance at critical moments or simply enable charities to try out new ideas. We also offer more than just financial support by guiding and mentoring individuals with a charitable vision as they make their dream a reality.

Two Temple Place is the focal point for many of our initiatives. It hosts many of our regular activities including the Engaging Experience Philanthropy Network (connecting business people with charities in need of specific skills), our partnership with the Fulbright Commission to develop philanthropy among its alumni, and marquee events for small charities that would otherwise not have the opportunity to access a similar setting. The house is also used commercially as an exclusive events venue, with all revenue earned supporting the work of the Trust.

As well as our charitable activities, we open Two Temple Place to the public for our annual Winter Exhibitions. These aim to raise awareness of the wonderful collections held by museums and galleries outside London and enable institutions around the UK to showcase what makes them special. In collaboration with the Courtauld Institute of Art, our exhibitions also give emerging curators a chance to be guided through their first solo show.

This publication is the first detailed work on the origins of Two Temple Place and its subsequent history. It has had many different roles in the last hundred years: we look forward to it supporting the Bulldog Trust achieve its charitable and cultural objectives in the twenty-first century.

Charles M R Hoare *Chairman of the Trustees, The Bulldog Trust*

ACKNOWLEDGEMENTS

On first encountering Two Temple Place a year ago, I was immediately seduced by its charms. The tours I gave when it opened to the public confirmed to me that there was a personal story lying behind the ornate and enigmatic decorative scheme. Discovering William Waldorf Astor and this extraordinary building by John Loughborough Pearson has led me down many paths in my research. For their help in a variety of ways I would like to thank Anthony Quiney, David Barrie, Simon Bradley, Ian Blatchford, John Liffen, Tilly Blyth, Nigel Wilkins, Javis Gurr, Daniel Robbins, Bridget Howlett, Peter Gunn, Alice Bray, Roger Bettridge, Sally Mason, Richard Hunt and the staff at the RIBA. Regarding Astor's country house, Cliveden, whose collections are now in the care of the National Trust, my thanks are due to Alastair Laing for early introductions and advice. I also thank John Waxman and Librarian Mark Purcell who facilitated my work. Also at the National Trust Lucy Porten and Tania Adams aided in various ways. Max Bryant 'took the tour' and provided invaluable assistance in identifying the Shakespearean sources. Most importantly, Julius Bryant has, as ever, been a huge help, especially in reading and commenting on my text. Thanks to the richness of the material about Two Temple Place, I plan further publications on the building and its unusual owner, William Waldorf Astor.

This book aims to be a readable, modestly sized monograph. Without the support of staff and trustees at Two Temple Place, the research project would not have been launched. To the vision of Mary Rose Gunn, Chief Executive of The Bulldog Trust, I would like to pay tribute. I also thank former Development Manager Madeleine Reid who enthusiastically dealt with queries and moved the project on in its early stages. Others at Temple Place have provided assistance, including Charles Arkwright, Hannah Jordan and Jackie Brewster. Julian Nieman's photographs have made the house come alive. My warm thanks are also due again to Colin Grant and to Adam Thorpe, whose efforts have made the book such an attractive publication. Both Baron Astor of Hever and Viscount Astor of Hever Castle answered key queries, and for that I am most grateful.

Barbara Bryant *Highgate, November 2012*

CONTENTS

INTRODUCTION 6

THE PATRON 11

THE BUILDING OF THE ASTOR
ESTATE OFFICE 17

EXTERIOR DECORATION 31

THE INTERIOR 41

ASTOR AT THE ESTATE OFFICE:
'THERE, AT LEAST, I AM SAFE' 78

THE ESTATE OFFICE AFTER ASTOR 86

NOTES 92

INTRODUCTION

Situated in a quiet corner of Temple Place, overlooking the Thames from London's Victoria Embankment, stands a remarkable building (fig. 1). Characterised variously as Gothic, Tudor, Elizabethan, Jacobean or Renaissance in style, it strikes a romantic note with its picturesque silhouette and beguiling exterior decoration.

Closer observation reveals it is not historicist, however, but very much a building of the 1890s. Walking through the door, one enters a splendid world of luxurious materials and finely crafted, endlessly inventive decoration. Today this is the home of the Bulldog Trust charity, but originally the house had a rather different purpose as the estate office of William Waldorf Astor, one of the richest men in the world at the end of the nineteenth century.

With the fortunes of the Astor family based on real estate in New York City, it seems only fitting that William Waldorf enjoyed an exceptional relationship with architecture. As his grand hotels and apartment blocks went up on one side of the Atlantic, Astor bought, built or rebuilt his way through southern England. His legacy includes not only Two Temple Place but also his radical changes to Cliveden in Buckinghamshire, 18 Carlton House Terrace in London and, later, Hever Castle in Kent. The building that we can now see and explore at Two Temple Place rose swiftly in the 1890s. Completed late in 1895, it served as the headquarters for the Astor Estate and as a private retreat for Astor himself. It played this role for just under twenty-five years. After that its fortunes followed various paths, as different owners took its uniqueness under their wing and generally maintained it with exemplary care.

Over the years its virtues have attracted architectural historians such as Sir John Betjeman, who in 1971 sang its praises as a 'little masterpiece'.[1] Nikolaus Pevsner hailed it as 'a perfect gem' and in 1957 included the Astor Estate Office (then

'A perfect gem'
NIKOLAUS PEVSNER

FIG. 1
Two Temple Place in 2012

With its pristine exterior enclosing a beautifully crafted interior, such allusions to sparkling jewels encased in a perfect container seem to hit the right note

headquarters of Smith & Nephew) in the first title featuring London in *The Buildings of England* series.[2] His approval may well have prompted its Grade II*-listed status, which came about in 1960. It first opened to the public very recently, its qualities having long remained in the shadows (but for a brief foray into the nation's living rooms via television in 1996, when the actor Ian McShane filmed his legal drama series *Madson* here). Even for those fortunate enough to have visited as guests, this strange structure has always remained an enigma. As we will see in this book, Two Temple Place has many stories to tell.

'CASTLE OF COMMERCE' AND ARTS AND CRAFTS MASTERPIECE

In descriptions of Two Temple Place it is striking how often the words, 'gem', 'jewel' and 'casket' occur. With its pristine exterior enclosing a beautifully crafted interior (fig. 2), such allusions to sparkling jewels encased in a perfect container seem to hit the right note. The architect John Loughborough Pearson had a deep understanding of how to integrate architecture and decorative arts in a unified ensemble. His exacting standards are reflected right through from his original drawings for the project in 1892–3 to the finished product, where every aspect of the stonework and joinery (even locksmithing) is precise and natural materials speak for themselves. Everywhere he deployed his 'quaint and fresh combination of Gothic and Renaissance ideas'.[3]

Pearson assembled a group of artist-craftsmen and gave them the opportunity of a lifetime – to produce their best work with no expense spared. William Silver Frith, Nathaniel Hitch, Thomas Nicholls, John Starkie Gardner and George Frampton rose to the challenge and created masterpieces of decorative art and design for the house. These men, of different generations, worked at a time when the arts and crafts were enjoying a new lease of life. In the 1880s and early 1890s, with the formation of the Art Workers' Guild and the staging of related exhibitions, the climate was right for a flowering of British design. This building both inside and out represents some of the finest work of the period, but we should remember that it was a building with a purpose: to serve as William Waldorf Astor's business premises, or what one contemporary called 'a castle of commerce'. Yet it was also much more than that: it was Astor's personal sanctuary, and all the decorative splendour reflected his astonishing wealth and unusual interests.

THE CREATION OF ASTOR'S OFFICE

To comprehend the building, one needs to understand William Waldorf Astor. For a newspaperman he had a remarkably bad press and still does, thanks to

FIG. 2
The gallery above the Staircase Hall
at Two Temple Place

his strange and prickly personality. Some of this is unjust. The story is far more interesting if one jettisons the preconceptions and looks at what the patron of Two Temple Place was trying to achieve. Astor died in 1919, but despite the passage of nearly one hundred years, his presence undeniably permeates this place. His passions, interests and artistic tastes account for the extraordinary interior scheme, which is so personal to him that it reads almost like his own autobiography.

However, one other element of his character and that of his chosen architect, John Loughborough Pearson, is relevant. Astor had a genuinely secretive nature, and Pearson, despite his eminence, avoided personal publicity. Although vast holdings of material relating to the Astor family exist in archives and libraries on both sides of the Atlantic, there is (so far) no known group of papers detailing this commission for the building of the estate office. We do not have Astor's own words for what he intended here, nor are there letters or direct comments from Pearson on this project.[4] Some interesting secondary sources give us a taste of the patron's thinking. Fortunately, an important collection of drawings by Pearson and his office for this commission survive in the Royal Institute of British Architects (figs 14, 15, 17, 60, 85), and other drawings and historic photographs fill out the story. Even with limitations, thanks to extensive contemporary discussion about Astor in the press and about the building itself, we can take that essential leap into the past and recreate the circumstances of its conception and reception.

Despite serious damage during World War II, the building survived throughout the twentieth century and into the next century – a matter for celebration. Its magnificent decorative scheme is largely intact so that we can explore Two Temple Place in all its facets as it exists today. This book seeks to draw out the hidden stories this building has to tell and bring it to life, but first it is necessary to step back and consider the patron himself.

Despite serious damage during World War II, the building survived throughout the twentieth century and into the next century – a matter for celebration

THE PATRON

'In himself and in the lonely life he led amid the environments he had acquired or created – surroundings partly noble and magnificent, partly fantastic and baroque – Lord Astor was an extraordinary and singular personality.' (From 'A Personal Impression of William Waldorf Astor, by a Friend', *The Times,* 1919[5])

William Waldorf (1848–1919; fig. 3) began life in New York City as the only child of John Jacob Astor III (1822–90). He had huge wealth at his disposal; even so, the Astors in the mid-nineteenth century were only two generations beyond the fur-trading founder of the dynasty, John Jacob I (1763–1848), who had left the village of Walldorf near Heidelberg in south-western German to try his luck across the Atlantic. This man amassed the family's money through trade in the far west of the United States. Due to sheer enterprise and financial acumen, he accrued great profits, which he ploughed into buying property on Manhattan Island.[6] William Waldorf was born in the very year his great-grandfather died. An only child, he read widely, indulging his intense interest in history and those individuals who shaped the past. His pastime of choice was chess, which he later viewed as an allegory of life. He received his early education at home followed by law studies at Columbia University in New York.

Travel in Europe had a huge impact on this insular young man. Initially, he accompanied his parents there, then he studied at Göttingen University and finally, in his early twenties, he went on his own independent 'grand tour'. In the 1860s he absorbed high culture, hearing Franz Liszt play, mixing with a bohemian set and visiting artists' studios, particularly sculptors such as Hiram Powers, who was based in Florence. Astor gravitated to Rome and tasted life as an artist, trying his hand at sculpture. The only known example of his work, *The Dying Amazon* (fig. 4), may well have been carried out under the tutelage of the American sculptor, William Wetmore Story, who was a focal point for the expatriate community in Rome. While in Italy, Astor had the great formative experience of his early life, when he fell in love with a mysterious young woman who is never named but is referred to much later in his highly selective memoir *Silhouettes* as 'The Princess of my Fairy Tale'.[7] Forbidden to marry her by his family, the twenty-one-year-old Astor was devastated and the memory of this beauty and their love for each other never left him. For forty years he carried a torch for her and later wrote movingly about the episode. This incident manifested itself in many other ways, as we shall see. These European experiences also endowed Astor with an understanding of art and culture; he avidly read histories of Italy, romances, and biographies of great leaders, developing a 'lurking fondness' for the Italian despots, the Borgias, Sforzas and Gonzagas. By this time Astor had mastered several languages. He became a true Romantic, as all of these rich experiences influenced his later outlook and his interest in the arts.

In 1870 Astor returned to New York City to work in the offices of the family's growing real-estate empire. His life lacked the colour Italy had provided, yet he had duties to perform as a member of a great business empire. His father, John Jacob Astor II, was beginning to relinquish control and expected his son to take over. Astor learned the trade but business bored him, so he embarked on a political career, standing for election to the New York state legislature as a Republican in 1877.[8] Perhaps he felt this life might offer more excitement, but he was singularly unsuited to the rough trade of politics and the provocative 'tobacco-spitting journalism' of the political scene at that time. Although he served in state government for two years, being in the public eye as 'an Astor' meant that he came in for endless personal criticism in the press. He considered a move to Washington DC and the national stage, but he lost two congressional elections and also the taste for that kind of public life.

In June 1878, during his brief political career, Astor married the nineteen-year-old Mary Dahlgren Paul (fig. 5), who came from a prominent family in Philadelphia. Although he later remarked that his father had chosen the bride for him, he had a companionable marriage with the softly spoken Mary, known to friends and family as Mamie. Her social graces and easy manner made up for his reticent ways. They were a handsome couple: he was over six feet tall, with strong features and blue eyes, and Mary's fashionable hair styles framed a sweet face. Two children were born in quick succession, a son, Waldorf, in 1879 and a daughter, Pauline, in 1880 (with another infant dying early the following year). Astor was still a young man, now in his early thirties, and after political disappointments he had to find a suitable course in life. In 1882 fate intervened when Astor was offered a prestigious political appointment in Rome – Chef de Mission in the Diplomatic Corps. Aged only thirty-four, he accepted with enthusiasm as one of the youngest men to have held this ministerial position.

Fig. 4
William Waldorf Astor, *The Dying Amazon*, c.1870, marble sculpture in the gardens of Cliveden, Buckinghamshire

Famously, President Chester Arthur sent him on his way with instructions to 'Go and enjoy yourself, my dear boy, have a good time!'[9]

With this blessing, Astor left with his family for Rome, settling in the grand Palazzo Rospigliosi on the Quirinale hill and working at the legation near the Piazza di Spagna. As he later commented, 'my Government gave me so little to do that I was able to lead a free life, – Archaeology, pictures, Renaissance history, and excursions' to the Campagna. His passion for collecting classical sculpture began in these years.[10] In 1885 he commissioned a fellow American, Richard Saltonstall Greenhough, to sculpt portrait busts of himself and his wife (both now National Trust, Cliveden) in antique garb. Indulging his artistic inclinations in other ways, Astor took up writing and produced his first novel, *Valentino: An Historical Romance of the Sixteenth Century in Italy* (1885), centring on his favourite Renaissance anti-hero, Cesare Borgia, whose family had occupied the splendid Palazzo Rospigliosi three hundred years before. Several years later another fictional tale appeared, *Sforza: A Story of Milan* (1889), which he dedicated to 'my dear wife Mary'.

These years in Rome confirmed Astor's cosmopolitan tastes, but in 1885 the Italian idyll came to an end with a change in political masters in Washington. The Astors returned to New York; another son, John Jacob V, arrived in 1886, and a daughter, Gwendolyn, in 1889. When his father died in 1890, leaving him sole heir to the family fortune, which had built up since mid-century, William Waldorf Astor found himself the richest man in the world. But all was not well with the wider Astor clan, particularly when his imperious aunt, Caroline Schermerhorn Astor, declared herself to be 'THE Mrs Astor' in New York society. William Waldorf took umbrage for himself as much as for his wife, and this incident, along with his disenchantment with politics, sensitivity to press criticism and, it was rumoured, the fear of his children being kidnapped, prompted a plan to leave his homeland for good.

When William Waldorf Astor first arrived in London in the early 1890s, he intended nothing less than to reinvent himself completely. It would be a major project but one that he was well prepared to carry out. His great wealth meant no physical or material obstacle would ever deter him as he embarked on his far-reaching plan to live, act and be accepted as a member of the very highest echelons of British society. Travelling in his wake were his wife and young family, all destined to find their fates also locked into British life and culture. Central to Astor's project were the appropriate architectural settings for his new life. Here the story of Two Temple Place begins.

After a short trip in 1890–91, the Astors arrived to settle in England in autumn 1891. William Waldorf lost no time in establishing himself; temporary quarters at Lansdowne House in Berkeley Square (where he lived with his family and nineteen staff) gave way to ever more impressive residences. He rented the handsome country house, Cliveden, in Buckinghamshire (fig. 6) from the Duke of Westminster and in London took out a long lease on the largest and grandest mansion in Carlton House Terrace, at the nexus of prestige and influence with aristocratic and political neighbours as well as fellow millionaires. Astor also wanted to wield influence, and to that end, in 1892, one of his most conspicuous gestures was the acquisition of the well-known journal, *The Pall Mall Gazette*, a liberal paper he famously turned conservative, and its popular sister publication, *The Pall Mall Budget*. One journalist commented that, by purchasing the paper, Astor was like a 'fairy godfather' to the staff at the offices in Northumberland Street (off the Strand); nevertheless, he exercised full control, went in to work regularly, hired and fired summarily (and without warning), and dictated policy. He seemed to enjoy sparring with the group of dynamic young men he recruited to run the paper, including Lord Frederick Hamilton and Harry Cust, who became the editor. When Cust refused to print his boss's own fiction, Astor simply started up another related title in May 1893, *The Pall Mall Magazine,* which attracted well-regarded authors and nurtured emerging ones, such as H.G. Wells and Rudyard Kipling. In the course of the 1890s the *Gazette* became the best evening paper in London; as owner, Astor gained considerable influence and power with his aspirations growing accordingly. In 1893 he purchased Cliveden outright from its owner for a reported 1.25 million dollars. Like it or not, with such an extravagant act, Astor again found himself in the public eye, the subject of gossip and speculation of various kinds.

ASTOR'S EARLY LIFE IN LONDON

On arrival in London, William Waldorf Astor and his family made an immediate splash in society. He sought nothing less than full integration into aristocratic and royal circles, yet this quest progressed fitfully. Initially, no one would have had much idea about him as a person. The immensely rich, American ex-ambassador came to London intending to write books; indeed, his reputation as an author preceded him. Although today his books are routinely maligned, when published they were for the most part well received. He had submitted his first manuscript anonymously so that it would be read on its own merits. On its publication in London in 1886, the *Morning Post* assessed *Valentino* as the result of Astor's long residence in Italy and considered that its 'powerful portraits' of the Borgias allowed the reader to be transported back to the Renaissance era.[11]

FIG. 6
Cliveden, Buckinghamshire (National Trust)

In 1890 *The Pall Mall Gazette* reported that Astor 'thinks more of writing than he does of his enormous fortune, and is now travelling in Europe with the purpose of collecting material for a new novel'.[12]

This glow of literary status slowly evaporated, as a series of social gaffes, all of his own making, beset Astor. With a conversational style sometimes limited to the words 'Yes' and 'No', his abrupt manner called attention to itself. He reserved particular dislike for the press in his former home city, and in July 1892 he went so far as to allow his representatives in London to announce his death, so that he could see how the newspapers in the States would write about his life. Even when this hoax was quickly corrected by cable, many journals went ahead for commercial reasons, concluding 'that there was more to be made by killing Astor than by keeping him alive',[13] which only confirmed his belief that the press in New York despised him.

For a time in the early 1890s life for the Astors did go according to plan. His wife Mary was much liked and found her place in society easily, mixing with those close to royal circles, although it was also rumoured that she pined for her homeland. In London her famous jewels often drew notice, particularly a French diamond coronet comb with a provenance from Louis XIV, which she wore to one of Queen Victoria's gatherings in 1893. It was said that Mary had 'a pretty taste for jewels ... especially for those worn by famous women',[14] which her husband seems to have encouraged. Astor's elder daughter, Pauline, was always his favourite; the younger one, Gwendolyn, had serious health problems. He sent his sons, Waldorf and John, to Eton, where they excelled at sport. Life seemed in place for Astor. His purchase of *The Pall Mall Gazette* made him a key newspaper proprietor in London. He could afford to indulge himself, and this was just the moment when he commissioned the Estate Office.

THE BUILDING OF THE ASTOR ESTATE OFFICE

Parallel with Astor's activities in acquiring prestigious properties and newspapers was his own family business. He had to superintend the activities of the Astor Estate in New York from his new home in London.

Almost immediately, certainly by 1892, he commissioned an estate office. He might have rented space in central London, but instead the idea of a whole new property, purpose-built, with modern conveniences and the requisite security took precedence. Such a course allowed Astor also to exercise his own aesthetic preferences; building the estate office became a pleasant hobby for him, one where he indulged his love of literature, history and art.

THE SITE: VICTORIA EMBANKMENT

Astor bought a parcel of land on Victoria Embankment, at the eastern edge of Westminster before it merges with the City of London (fig. 8). Just to the east was the winding Milford Lane and, beyond that, the area known as the Temple, a great complex containing gardens and attendant buildings for the barristers of the Middle Temple. Here, with its incongruously high, steeply pitched roof, stood the Middle Temple Library built in 1861 by Henry R. Abraham (fig. 9; destroyed 1941), whose mostly routine architectural output has not created a lasting reputation.

In the eighteenth century the land where Two Temple Place is now located fronted onto the river Thames, in an area that contained Hutchinson's and Milford Lane Wharves and related trades; later, in the mid-nineteenth century, prior to the creation of the Embankment, it was on or near Essex Street Wharves, site of Gwynne and Company, a family concern of civil engineers and inventors of various types of pumping machines and heavy equipment, such as James Gwynne's patented improved centrifugal pump and a machine for 'breaking, crushing and reducing stones and other substances'.[15] With the massive public project of the embanking of the Thames in the 1860s (fig. 7), most of these

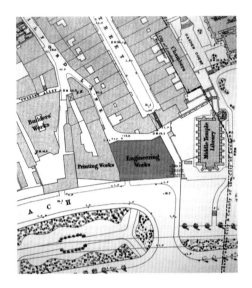

FIG. 8 ABOVE
Map showing in red Gwynne's engineering works on the site later bought by William Waldorf Astor (reproduction from Ordnance Survey map of 1875 with kind permission of the Ordnance Survey)

FIG. 7 LEFT
Construction of the Embankment, engraving from the *Illustrated London News,* August 1864. The future site of the Astor Estate Office appears to the far left, just in front of the Middle Temple Library

17

FIG. 9 LEFT
View across the river with the
Middle Temple Library and
Gwynne's on the left, 1861,
engraving from a contemporary
periodical

businesses were swept away. The land then extended some 200 feet (61 metres) beyond the original shore line. In fact, on the spot of Two Temple Place (still then named The Approach and later Approach Road) some humble structures remained for just over twenty years, until Astor's purchase. The front line of the plot coincided with the original line of the river Thames; everything beyond that was reclaimed land.

The new Embankment allowed for great improvements in transport, with trams and underground trains, and drainage, as well as the creation of public amenities, such as Victoria Gardens, a modern pleasure ground for Londoners complete with a bandstand; an increasing population of commemorative sculpture depicted praiseworthy individuals, including John Stuart Mill (1878) by Thomas Woolner, close to the Astor Estate Office. Beautification of the Embankment included handsome bronze lamp standards for the electric lights and plans for sculptural decoration of the piers. The whole area had the feel of a modern metropolis with new architecture, such as the nearby Arundel Hotel, Surrey House and Norfolk House, erected in the mid-1880s by James Dunn, and the Howard Hotel, finished in 1894, all in the prevailing Gothic Revival style then gripping the English architectural establishment. By far the most striking edifice was G.F. Bodley and Thomas Garner's London School Board Offices (1872–6, demolished

FIG. 10 RIGHT
London School Board Offices,
Victoria Embankment Gardens,
with the edge of the Astor Estate
Office to the far right, c.1900
(photograph reproduced by
permission of English Heritage,
NMR)

1929) in the contemporary 'Queen Anne' revival idiom with its white stone and red brick-banded facade. It had a modest presence until two enlargements, the last by R.W. Edis in 1891–3 (fig. 10), transformed it into a massive building that dominated Approach Road, yet next to it was a shanty-like accumulation of low structures, warehouses belonging to Gwynne's engineering works, and this unlikely spot is the one Astor purchased.

So why did this area appeal to Astor? As a trained lawyer himself, he would have appreciated the position near the Middle Temple, one of the ancient inns of court, as a setting for his own offices; as someone with an acute sense of history, he would have been attracted to the romantic tales associated with nearby Temple Gardens, such as the plucking of the white and red roses representing the two sides in the Wars of the Roses. Essex Street and Essex Steps, still a charming backwater of the area, also held key historical associations as the site of the gardens of Essex House, residence of Queen Elizabeth I's favourite, Robert Devereaux; indeed, the whole area south of the Strand had housed the great mansions of the Tudor era with their gardens extending down to the Thames. This part of London resonated with the past. Yet, with the creation of the Embankment, it had stepped decisively into modern times, and that had a dual appeal for a man who considered himself a historical writer, while running one of the most extensive business empires of the time. For Astor, the writer and noted bibliophile, this area, in particular Milford Lane, a centre for second-hand booksellers, possessed further cachet. In practical terms it was in walking distance of *The Pall Mall Gazette's* offices,[16] where Astor spent much time, and his own town residence at Carlton House Terrace. Above all, this area had a secluded feel, somewhat removed from the bustling and busy Embankment with its trams and buses and the Thames with its paddle steamers and piers. The plot was hemmed in by the School Board Offices and the Middle Temple Library, lending it a sense of enclosure.[17] Given Astor's obsession with privacy, he seems to have envisaged his own small fortress occupying this modest site.

THE ARCHITECT:
JOHN LOUGHBOROUGH PEARSON (1817–97)

A senior member of the architectural profession in London, J.L. Pearson had enjoyed a long and productive career spanning six decades (fig. 11). By the 1890s his reputation as one of the great Gothic Revivalists of the century was secure; indeed, many considered him to be 'the founder of the modern school of Gothic architecture'.[18] In the 1840s, early in his career, he followed Pugin but later established his own virtues. Best known for St Augustine's, Kilburn (1870–97), and his magnum opus, Truro Cathedral (1878 onwards), Pearson treated

The whole area had the feel of a modern metropolis with new architecture, such as the nearby Arundel Hotel, Surrey House and Norfolk House

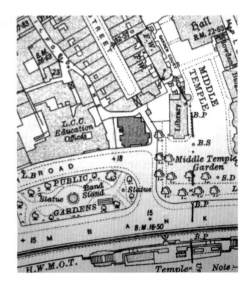

interior space in a free and dramatic manner, particularly through his use of vaulting. Always one for clarity of plan, he was equally involved with the finer aspects of each commission, as one contemporary observed: 'He attended to every detail himself, and liked to design the furniture and ornaments … to be used in his buildings.'[19] This love of ornament and decorative detailing comes out vividly in the Astor Estate Office.

In 1879 he succeeded George Gilbert Scott in the prestigious post of Surveyor to the Fabric of Westminster Abbey. In following through on Scott's plan to restore the north transept and then alter the medieval Westminster Hall, Pearson encountered the preservationist lobby of the day, the Society for the Protection of Ancient Buildings, with its leading light William Morris taking up arms against him in a pamphlet, *Concerning Westminster Abbey*, published in 1893. Unlike Morris, Pearson had no taste for public squabbles. He was nearing seventy by then and suffered in the public spotlight. It is a statement of his very high reputation that these events did not detract from a career that had been capped by the Gold Medal of the Royal Institute of British Architects in 1880. Devoted to his work and his studies of architectural history, Pearson had great knowledge, which he deployed with a light touch in his buildings, especially towards the end of his career.

His blameless personal life held no secrets but it did have one great sadness – he had been married for only three years before his wife Jemima died of typhoid fever in 1865,[20] leaving him the father of an infant son. Frank Loughborough Pearson (1864–1947) grew up to become his father's business associate in the architectural practice and continued well into the twentieth century with his own career, much of it taking up the reins of working for Astor at Cliveden, Carlton House Terrace and especially at Hever Castle in Kent (from 1903 onwards),[21] where he played a key role in the restoration and re-presentation of the estate. Friends considered J.L.Pearson 'a fine specimen of the English gentleman', courtly in his manner and reticent in his ways. A writer commented that 'he went little into any society but that of his club and his fellow-artists'.[22] His scholarly interests suited such groups as the Society of Antiquaries, where he had been a fellow since 1853. For his own home and office he chose to live in a townhouse on Mansfield Street, north of Oxford Street, designed by Robert Adam, the great architect of the eighteenth century.

How the seventy-four-year-old Pearson, a man of devout religious faith, and the forty-three-year-old millionaire and non-believer, William Waldorf Astor, came into contact around 1891 is not known, but with Pearson's eminent reputation, and perhaps also due to his low public profile, this unlikely pair hit it off. Anecdotally, there is an account of how Astor had to work hard to get Pearson to accept the commission for the estate office on the Embankment. Yet even though his chosen architect was well into old age, Pearson maintained a busy schedule, taking on new commissions such as the Middlesex Hospital Chapel (1890–93) and seeing through ongoing major works. As one of the foremost ecclesiastical architects in the country, he was not perhaps the obvious choice for a secular building in London, but it seems it was more a matter of patron and architect making a genuine connection with each other, although the deeper nature of that connection seems destined to remain opaque due to a lack of any documentation recording their contact. Both men valued their privacy and both were dedicated bibliophiles. Pearson, within his very much more modest means, amassed a good collection of architectural treatises and related works.[23] Astor collected on a much wider scale, as we shall see. Pearson would also have understood Astor's requirements for a new structure to serve a unique purpose and, as an architect, would surely have been stimulated by the challenge of this unusual building type – not a house, yet not an office block (fig. 13).

Significantly, money was no object. Astor gave Pearson 'a free hand to erect a perfect building irrespective of cost'.[24] The ultimate cost of the building was said to have been £250,000 (which equates to well over £10 million in today's money). Pearson's taste for rich materials is evident in many of his projects, as seen in his fondness for marble floors in varied colours and fine wood and stone carving by his regular team of artistic collaborators. Here, at the site that Astor had presented him with, he had leave to include the richest and most luxurious materials, use the best craftsmen and create the most extraordinary decorative scheme imaginable, because William Waldorf Astor required nothing less than the best.

THE BRIEF

What kind of building did Pearson produce for Astor? First and foremost, it was to be an office for the operations of the Astor Estate. Some notification reached the public press by May 1893: 'William Waldorf Astor intends to make London his headquarters in future for business as well as social purposes. Accordingly he has purchased a vacant piece of land on the Embankment, and will shortly erect a large office which will accommodate a staff of upward of thirty clerks.'[25] Due to the nature of such a building, certain aspects of the plan had priority: a grand entrance; a large open office area; several separate rooms for senior staff; and the usual practical areas below stairs. Safety and security played their role in the architectural scheme – a massive strongroom sat in the centre of the basement

FIG. 13
Two Temple Place, street facade

22

Astor gave Pearson 'a free hand to erect a perfect building irrespective of cost'

level, an additional strongroom was situated on the first floor, and there was at least one other safe near the ground-floor offices.

Central to the whole plan was Astor's own domain on the main floor where he would receive guests and employees, conduct his business and, as it turned out, enjoy his own leisure pursuits. This space had to have prominence, dignity and luxury commensurate with his position. Indeed, the other significant feature of the plan was the Staircase Hall. As this was the route important visitors would take on their way to see Astor, it possessed extraordinary richness of material and decoration. Beyond these factors, there were two other features particular to the patron – a library and a modestly sized but richly decorated bedroom (no longer extant).

THE BUILDING OF 1893–6: EXTERIOR

Conversations between Astor and Pearson must have taken place in early 1892, because by June Pearson and his office on Mansfield Street had produced a few attractive presentation drawings for the exterior and interior (figs 14, 15, 54, 60) with more following in 1893 (fig. 17). These are fully finished with coloured washes. By this time the scheme was almost entirely worked out and remained virtually unchanged through to building, with the exception of some refinement of the decorative elements. Many more drawings in 1893–5 aided in the working process. Pearson had to deal with the challenges of a restricted and relatively small, irregularly shaped site (fig. 12), as well as accommodating the variety of spaces necessary in a structure that served as Astor's personal headquarters and as a working office for the estate. Pearson's architectural drawings permit a clear understanding of the structure as built – a triumphant combination of simplicity of plan and elaboration of ornament.

The Astor Estate Office comprises two storeys, although it gives the impression of a much larger structure due to the broad and simple lines of Pearson's composition. Photographs show the positioning of the building close to Abraham's 'Cockney Gothic' Middle Temple Library, with only the narrow space of Milford Lane between them (fig. 16). In a nicely judged way Pearson took the crenellated line directly across from the library to the estate office, thus establishing a sense of the continuity between the two structures and allowing his building to partake of the Gothicising spirit of neighbouring architecture. Even at the time observers commented how the building 'architecturally harmonizes with the Temple and is taken by most passers by for part of it'.[26] Viewed frontally, the main body of Pearson's structure is symmetrical, yet the whole is animated by its picturesque silhouette, with battlements and high tower-like chimneys conjuring

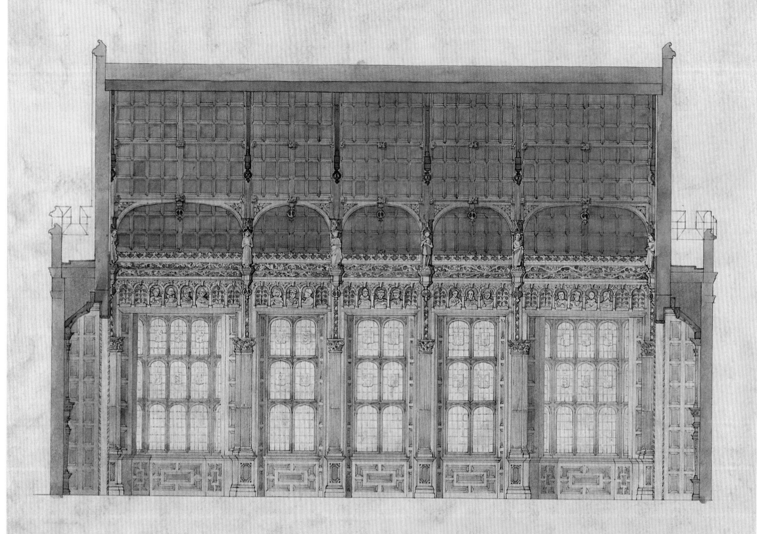

ASTOR ESTATE OFFICE
VICTORIA EMBANKMENT
SECTIONS OF GREAT ROOM
SCALE ¼ IN = 1 FT

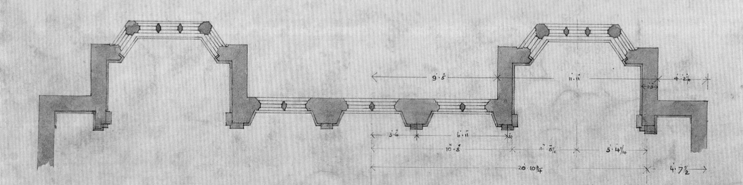

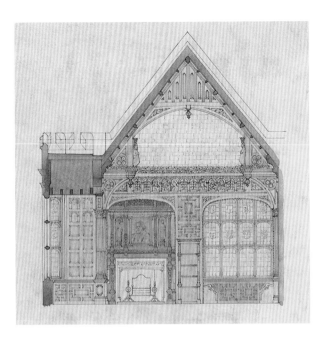

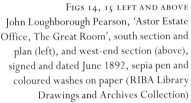

FIGS 14, 15 LEFT AND ABOVE
John Loughborough Pearson, 'Astor Estate
Office, The Great Room', south section and
plan (left), and west-end section (above),
signed and dated June 1892, sepia pen and
coloured washes on paper (RIBA Library
Drawings and Archives Collection)

FIG. 16 ABOVE RIGHT
The Astor Estate Office with the Middle
Temple Library on the right, from the sale
catalogue, 1920 (Centre for
Buckinghamshire Studies)

up romantic associations with the past. At the top of the structure, poised on a wrought-iron pyramidal pedestal, a golden-coloured copper weathervane in the form of a ship caps the roof line. Seen against the sky, this fanciful object sets the tone for a building where the decoration itself communicates directly to the viewer.

Built of Portland stone, the wide plain areas of the facade bear the traces of Pearson's famously meticulous treatment of stone surfaces, with his customary 'dressing' of this area to give an almost painterly quality.[27] The exterior parallel to the street makes the most of large mullioned windows on the projecting oriel bays and flat surfaces, letting the light in for both the lower floor (where the office was positioned) and the upper Great Hall, Astor's own domain. Placement of the building on the confined site was carefully considered: by pushing the structure to one side, the resulting space on the other allowed for the creation of a stately courtyard in front of the entrance facade.[28] One enters through an elaborate pair of iron gates with decorated piers, topped with carved urns and an armorial shield (this is now changed), giving a proper sense of occasion to an arrival into the environs of the estate office.

The western entrance facade of the building shows more irregularity with a projecting chimney, little windows and tiny turret, which are exactly matched on the other side, acting like bookends to buttress the horizontal expanse of the main body of the building. Tall chimneys reveal Pearson's penchant for towers and

spires, evident in his church designs, to counterbalance the mass of the building. Across the forecourt another large bay on the upper level displays the reverse of an elaborate stained-glass window. As seen in the drawing (fig. 17), the portico entrance with a flight of splayed balustraded steps is given special significance through its decoration (fig. 19), which initially included sculpted recumbent lions. Later this plan gave way to lamp standards incorporating bronze sculptures and electric lights, which are topped with further sculptural embellishment in the form of miniature model ships, echoing the one high up on the weathervane. The no-longer-extant heavy bronze doors decorated with brass would have enhanced the sense of enclosure and secrecy within. Filling the pediment above the doorway itself was a sculpture group with a central panel carved with the armorial bearings of the Astor family (fig. 18). The words, 'The Estate Office of John Jacob Astor', were carved in the stone lintel above the door. It is worth noting that the patron insisted that the proper name of the building made explicit reference to the founder of the Astor dynasty: it was not his estate office but that of his grandfather, and this familial theme continued in other areas of the house, as the owner implied that his family firm had its own pedigree.

Beyond the portico a short projecting wing closed off the courtyard area. This wing was extremely plain in contrast to the more ornate treatment of the main body of the building. With its simple gabled roof and lack of decorative string course or crenellation, it looked like it belonged to another building, yet on the first floor this area housed Astor's bedroom. One might have thought that

FIGS 18, 19 ABOVE AND RIGHT
Entrance facade and portico (detail above), December 1895, photograph by Bedford Lemere & Co. (reproduced by permission of English Heritage, NMR)

FIG. 17 ABOVE LEFT
John Loughborough Pearson, 'Astor Estate Office, West Elevation', dated 8 May 1893, pen and blue ink on linen-backed tracing paper (RIBA Library Drawings and Archives Collection)

such a space would be the occasion for even more elaborate decoration, and on the inside it certainly had that, but here on the exterior it almost seemed as if Astor sought an unostentatious effect as a statement of his desire for privacy. It even appeared as if the main body of the building, facing forwards onto the street, acted as a protective bulwark against the prying eyes of Astor's imagined enemies. This side of the building was heavily damaged in the bombing in July 1944 and was rebuilt, as will be discussed more fully below.

Fine ironwork surrounds the entire building, continuing all around to the side on Milford Lane. Not merely decorative, this fence helped to establish the perimeter against any potential intruders – Astor's obsession with security was ever present. The eastern side elevation (fig. 20), which would only be seen from close-up, had a stained-glass window to match the one on the main facade. The wall surface and prominent windows step in and out around the corner to the back of the structure. Here the plain wall gives way to a tower containing the back staircase and rising from ground level to well above the roof line, its smooth surface studded with a few lancet-like windows. This elegant curved form is a surprising feature in what would have been a dark enclosed area, but presumably a well-trod one, as pedestrians then and now hurry along to Essex Steps at this point. The staircase tower perfectly finishes off the structure with a flourish. In all aspects of the physical design of the building Pearson's famed sense of proportion and balance is evident.

STRUCTURE AND SECURITY

Pearson turned to his frequent collaborator, John Thompson of Peterborough, for the structural work.[29] Thompson, who had previously worked with George Gilbert Scott, carried out Pearson's rebuilding of portions of the cathedral in his home town from the early 1880s onwards. A reliable hand with the Gothic style due to a wide practice in church building and restoration, he also had the experience to undertake the heavy structural work that needed to be done. At Temple Place, given the instability of a site that was once on the edge of the Thames, deep excavations of some 30–40 feet (9–12 metres) down were required to lay the foundations. Precautions were taken to prevent flooding. According to Pearson's son, it was only under special conditions that floods might occur – spring tides combined with strong north or north-easterly winds.[30] An automatic valve mechanism backed up with an electric signal warned of the potential influx of water into the drains. Other practical matters, supervised by the foreman Mr F. Oxley, were part of the project, such as the fireproof floors and fire hydrants fitted on each floor, as well as a central-heating system.

FIG. 20
Eastern elevation from Milford Lane

29

A set of particular requirements made this project unique. Integral to the construction of the building was provision for two heavily protected strongrooms, as well as other safes in the offices. The secondary staircase, contained in the circular turreted tower, winds down to the basement (fig. 21). Here the plan included a range of functional areas such as kitchens, scullery, lesser offices and bedrooms for servants and other staff. The entire middle of this storey contained an enormous 20-by-20-foot (6.1 x 6.1-metre) 'Strong Room' with Portland cement and granite flooring laid on solid concrete, and its entrance marked by steel-lined oak-panelled doors. This space (called a 'Record Room' on Pearson's original drawing) had to be impregnable, as it contained accounts and securities for the management of the Astor Estate. Astor ordered an elaborate safe door from Chubb, the premier supplier of security equipment. In March 1894 they installed this 6½-foot (2-metre) behemoth, the first of several safety items custom-made for the office. Indeed, Astor's obsession with privacy fuelled his zealous patronage of Chubb's, as he continually ordered new safes and shifted others from property to property with demands that it was 'very urgent'. At one point he insisted that a safe be moved at night from one nearby office to the new building on the Embankment. By early 1895 most of these security measures were in position, even Astor's 'Private Vault', on the upper floor. This room was lined with steel plates weighing nearly a ton each and had a complicated locking device.[31] Such a heavy metal structure in this position of the house had a knock-on effect on the construction. The entrance hall on the ground floor in its original configuration had to be crowded with strong pillars required to support the strongroom and vault above. Once completed, Astor slept easily in the knowledge that his office was 'believed to be the strongest building in London after the Bank of England'.[32]

FIG. 21
Floor plan of the basement of the Astor
Estate Office, from the sale catalogue, 1920
(Centre for Buckinghamshire Studies)

EXTERIOR DECORATION

The great numbers of Gothic Revival churches erected throughout the nineteenth century required expert artist-craftsmen who could embellish the interiors and produce triptychs, reredoses, figural sculpture and other carved decorations.

Pearson's architecture, whether secular or ecclesiastical, had always featured integral decoration, and, as a result, over his long career he had gathered together a group of highly skilled individuals essential to fulfilling his view of architecture as a 'comprehensive art'.[33] Astor was therefore able to benefit from an architect who had a ready team, most based in London. Pearson always retained overall control down to the smallest detail, as is known from his work on other projects.[34] Many of the design elements would have been his own with instructions given to the art workers. Yet we also have to assume that these individuals had some of their own creative input. Each part of the building was in effect delegated to one person.

For the exterior carving on the front facade (fig. 22) that man was Nathaniel Hitch (1845–1938), an architectural sculptor and modeller based in Vauxhall. By the mid-1880s Pearson was employing Hitch in most of his major projects, including Truro Cathedral,[35] Westminster Hall and Westminster Abbey, where he carved the tympanum of the north transept, completed in 1892, at just the time of the Astor Estate Office commission.[36] Hitch, who was proficient in stone and wood carving, came up via the craftsman route, having started out as an apprentice with Farmer and Brindley, a firm of architectural sculptors in Lambeth also involved with making church furnishings. Eventually, he joined Thomas Nicholls, who had served as the main architectural sculptor in projects from 1860 onwards for the architect William Burges.[37] Nicholls, as discussed later, took on the role of senior figure in the Astor Estate Office project. Yet, for all his journeyman beginnings, Hitch was said to have a scholarly attitude to his craft. Pearson must have valued this, since he entrusted much of the carving at the Astor Estate Office to Hitch, including the key arena of the Great Room.

FIG. 23 LEFT
Detail of stone panel on the side
of the oriel windows; carving here
and in figs 24–6 by Nathaniel Hitch

FIG. 24 BELOW
Detail of window decoration

On the exterior a frieze with trigylphs and Tudor roses becomes more elaborate as it crosses the oriel windows and runs around the entire building like an ornate belt. Decoration is focused on the oriel windows, giving prominence to these elements in the overall composition of the facade. The main panels of carved stone show a sinuous display of oak leaves and vines emerging from a cornucopia-like urn topped with fruit (fig. 24). To the side two winged seahorses tethered to the edges of the stone panel seem to shriek in vigorous fashion (fig. 23). The urns seen in these panels were repeated in even larger and more ornate scale on the entrance gate piers, but these no longer survive.[38] Hitch produced some fifteen 'blind gargoyles', each one different, to top the drainpipes (fig. 25). Beaten-lead rainwater heads also take on grotesque shapes. All these fantastical creatures seem to burst forwards from their designated position high above street level, continually varying the silhouette against the sky. At the side another bizarre hybrid animal, part lion, part serpent, emerges from an oak-leafed enclosure, twisting around the edge of the building and glowering down at anyone below daring to look up (fig. 26). Hitch's contributions create an overall effect that is vividly alive and not conventional at all.[39] All the ornament he executed seems to pulsate with a real sense of energy.

The decorative ironwork was in the hands of another artist-craftsman, John Starkie Gardner (1845–1930), who had a scholarly interest in the history of his medium. As a young man, he travelled abroad and studied geology and botany, creating a corpus of drawings that led to an understanding of design in nature. This outlook informed much of his later work. In 1885 he started his 'Art

Metal Work' firm with a forge in Lambeth, producing original work and dealing in the restoration of historic metalwork. He soon (1886) received a major commission from the Department of Science and Art in South Kensington to design the gates to the mews entrance at the side of the Victoria and Albert Museum on Exhibition Road. This project may have recommended him to Pearson, although the architect would certainly have been impressed that Gardner was already a well-published expert on ironwork and enamels.[40]

Gardner received the commission at the estate office for the exterior and interior metalwork. His beautiful railings (also listed as Grade II*) around the perimeter of the building survive (fig. 97, p. 88), as do the gates, although they are now set within different piers and lack the elaborate 'overthrow', a shield-like confection ornamented with a massive shell and leafage. The real flourish on the exterior of the estate office is the eye-catching weathervane on the roof: a historic ship mounted on a decorated finial (fig. 98, p. 89). Gardner's contribution here became one of the most noteworthy aspects of the building, attracting comment right from the beginning. The galvanised-steel vane supports a ship of beaten copper. Its fanciful shape actually had a specific meaning, as it took the form of a fifteenth-century Spanish vessel. Early writers identified it as Columbus's ship (the *Santa Maria*) from the famous voyage of 1492 and the discovery of America,[41] a historical episode that would have had particular significance for the expatriate Astor and establishes the American theme that recurs in the decorative scheme. Did he dictate its subject? So specific is the reference that we have to assume Astor requested it and that Pearson instructed Gardner to produce it. Thanks to his skill as an art metalworker, Gardner designed a miniature boat of such buoyancy that it seems to be sailing among the clouds in imaginary contrast to the solid stone structure below.

William Silver Frith (1850–1924),[42] like Hitch, played a major role at the Astor Estate Office with important contributions in wood and stone carving both inside and outside. His grand portico is now gone, but much else remains. Although he did not have the track record with Pearson that some of the other craftsmen did, Frith's reputation preceded him. Highly regarded as a teacher of sculpture, he was instrumental in setting up modelling classes for craftsmen at the South London School of Technical Art, succeeding the French sculptor Jules Dalou as master in 1880. Frith exhibited as a fine artist at the Royal Academy as well as being a stalwart member of the Art Workers' Guild from 1886. He was the architectural sculptor of choice for the architect Aston Webb on several major projects.[43] In 1892, at just the time he embarked on the Astor Estate Office, Frith lectured at the RIBA on the relation of sculpture to architecture, a subject

FIG. 25 ABOVE
Gargoyles

FIG. 26 RIGHT
Fantastical creature on the side of the building

FIG. 27 LEFT
Miniature galleon at full sail on top
of one of the entrance lamps

FIG. 28 RIGHT
Doorway and stairs of Two Temple
Place, with lamps by William
Silver Frith

on which he held strong beliefs. Sculpture was not subservient to a building but worked in concert with it. The properties of each material had to be carefully considered. Later he wrote about his objections to the term 'architectural decoration', 'for architecture worthy of the name does not require decoration'.[44]

Pearson assigned Frith the key area of the portico entrance to the estate office where the high level of sculptural embellishment in carved stone had a powerful impact. Much of this area does not survive (see below), but Frith's remarkable bronze lamp standards do. These two tall lamps stand at the bottom of the staircase leading to the main doorway (fig. 28). They were not in position immediately but provided the finishing touch to the house. Their elegant proportions and inventive figural groups of playful putti have always attracted attention;[45] indeed, the artist exhibited his working version of the group at the Royal Academy some years later in 1908, simply calling it *Model of a Lamp Standard*. A pair of seemingly ordinary pillar-style lamps topped by ornamental historic ships assume a delightful complexity with pairs of wingless androgynous putti, swags of garlands and some very unusual accessories. The freedom of handling and the naturalistic treatment of the figures bring this frivolous composition to life, but what do these little naked creatures represent?

Closer inspection shows that the lamps were making a point about the estate office, done with a humorous touch that was probably down to Frith himself.

The lamp to the right shows the leading putto holding to his (or her?) ear a single-pole magneto telephone (fig. 29), the earliest type produced by the Bell Telephone Company, which came into commercial use in the late 1870s.[46] Electrical wiring twists around the swags of leaves and trails down to the back of the lamp, where on a lower level a fellow putto grasps the phone, holding it upwards to speak into it and relay his voice down the wire. Next to this individual is the cylindrical transmitting device (fig. 30). On the second lamp a naked putto raises aloft an electric filament light bulb of a type in use in the 1890s (fig. 31). His companion below appears adjacent to an apparatus that may well be 'shocking coils', a stack of magnets with rotating coils, a popular, pseudo-medical electricity-generating device of the period.

In the 1880s the new phenomenon of electricity made its way into more and more buildings in the West End and the City. A central supply hub at nearby Holborn Viaduct had opened in 1882, and even nearer to the estate office was the station for the City of London Power Supply Company at Blackfriars, active from 1892 onwards. The excitement of this innovation gave rise to this unusual artwork. The celebratory pose of the left-hand figure suggests a quirky allegorical representation of the triumph of electricity to match the commemoration of telephonic communication in the other lamp. These themes refer to those heroic American inventors Thomas Edison and Alexander Graham Bell (a Scots-born, naturalised American), whose scientific achievements revolutionised daily life and business in Astor's own time. The lamps contained electric lights (still in working order today) illuminating the entrance of the estate office, and within the building the most up-to-date electronic equipment was installed. In this way the sculpture on view conveyed to the visitor that he was about to enter the premises of a thoroughly modern-day establishment.[47]

The point is made in a light-hearted manner with little naked children playing with modern technological equipment, yet there were also references to the past with the placement of two historic ships on top of the glass-enclosed electric lamps. Each miniature galleon sails along on the waves (fig. 27). Such incongruous details must have had a specific meaning. Matched with Columbus's ship on the weathervane on the roof, they seem to be the other two ships on the journey to America; certainly, the two differing shapes of these ships are both caravel types. The nautical theme almost certainly refers back to the Astor family's history, since the founder of the dynasty sailed from Europe to the New World to make his fortune, a concept contained and commemorated in Pearson's building.

FIGS 29, 30 LEFT
Lower part of the
entrance lamp with
the two putti on the
phone (above) and
detail of the speaking
putto with the
transmitter (below)

FIG. 31 RIGHT
Putto on the
other lamp holding
a light bulb

THE INTERIOR

FIG. 33 ABOVE
Ground-floor (top) and first-floor (above) plans from the sale
catalogue, 1920 (Centre for Buckinghamshire Studies)

FIG. 32 LEFT
View up the staircase to the gallery and stained-glass skylight

ENTRANCE, OFFICE AND STAIRCASE HALL

Plans for the original layout of the estate office enable us to imagine what it was like to go into the building in the 1890s (fig. 33). On passing beyond the heavy bronze entrance doors, the early visitor had a choice of two routes. The vestibule is now different, but originally the ordinary individual with business to transact waited on an oak bench here before being escorted into the ground-level office (to the right) on the southern side of the building. This room was a well-managed functional area, subdivided into separate sections, with ample light for the clerical work that went on – today it is all one space called the Lower Gallery (fig. 34).[48] At the far end of the room one separate office housed Astor's trusted business manager and solicitor, John Coode Adams, who was a key individual in the running of the estate. Back areas included a boardroom (now divided into two rooms) and further offices. Panelled in oak, these areas were not ornamented in any unusual way apart from a long, wrought grille of polished steel made by Starkie Gardner, which sat on top of the low bank of cabinets that ran down the middle of the main room.[49] This grille, an unusually decorative security device, effectively separated any outsider from the working staff and from making any progress into the inner office.

A completely different experience awaited important visitors, family and friends, who proceeded along the main route into the building, straight on through the vestibule and into the grand double-height area of the Staircase Hall (fig. 35). This space impressed the minute one crossed the threshold, with a sensory assault of gorgeous materials, rich carving and literary references. It was a clear statement to mark the beginning of Astor's personal domain, and his choices are everywhere evident. The brilliantly coloured inlaid marble floor (fig. 36) evokes ancient structures like the Pantheon and the medieval Cosmatesque pavements of Roman churches, indicating that Astor, who had resided in Rome in the early 1880s, knew of these historic architectural displays. Pearson shared this interest; on his brief tour of Italy in 1874 he sketched the floors of some churches in Rome in watercolour.[51] In England the best-known example of this ancient work is at Westminster Abbey where Pearson was surveyor. He sought to incorporate modern versions of these displays in his own architectural interiors, as at Truro and Peterborough Cathedrals, but such effects could only be achieved when funds were available for the acquisition of the wide variety of richly coloured marbles necessary to create the decorative floors.

Equally important was a craftsman who specialised in such work, and here Pearson employed Robert Davison of the Decorative Art Studio on Marylebone Road to supervise the marble work throughout the building.[52] Davison had proved himself at Truro with the pavements 'of varied foreign marbles of different tints' and an elaborate font using a diverse accumulation of exotically named stones – red marble, fossil marble, vert des Alpes, giallo antico and breccia rosso antico, among others.[53] In the Staircase Hall at Two Temple Place the reds of the porphyry contrast with green jaspers and onyx in an increasingly complex pattern of circles and octagonals that are enclosed in various shapes and edged with curved elements composed of even smaller pieces of marble. The ornamental possibilities of rare coloured and veined marble, when cut into a variety of shapes and placed in intricate arrangements, produced a luxurious effect redolent of ancient Rome and the more ornate interiors of late medieval churches such as Santa Maria Maggiore. On one side of the room the powerful fireplace dominates. With paired green marble columns supporting a cornice,

Fig. 35 right
The Staircase Hall

Fig. 34 below
The Lower Gallery

its strong architectural form is further animated by the irregularly veined effect of the pavonazzetto marble, so named because its sometimes multi-coloured striations suggested the feathers of a peacock.

In the Staircase Hall the visitor gazes from the colourful effects of the floor directly up to a splendid stained-glass skylight with the date 1895 prominent in the centre panel (fig. 37). This detail commemorates the completion of the project. The rich red mahogany wood with elaborate balustrades marks the staircase out as a special feature as it rises through three levels. It is at this point that the main impetus of the decorative scheme reveals itself. The building embodied literature in a way entirely personal to William Waldorf Astor. Indeed, few, if any, of his visitors could have understood its symbolism, and we may imagine he delighted in expounding on it to favoured guests.

On the staircase the newel posts are ornamented with carved figures showing characters from the French novel, *Les Trois Mousquetaires* (1844–5) by Alexandre Dumas, known as Dumas *père* (figs 38–45).[54] Reputedly considered by Astor as the 'finest novel ever written',[55] *The Three Musketeers* is a rousing historical tale set in early seventeenth-century France that recounts the adventures of d'Artagnan, a young man from provincial Gascony who travels to Paris intent

FIG. 37 RIGHT
The stained-glass skylight dated 1895

FIG. 36 BELOW
The marble floor in the hall

FIG. 38
The d'Artagnan figure at the
bottom of the stairs seen from
the vestibule

on joining Louis XIII's famed band of swordsmen fighters. Taken up by those he strives to emulate, Athos, Porthos and Aramis, d'Artagnan fights duels in a series of heroic encounters, helps to save the reputation of Queen Anne of Austria and ends up a fully fledged member of the company of musketeers. The book, originally issued in instalments in the periodical press (much like Dickens's contemporaneous novels), is a rip-roaring sequence of adventurous escapades, complete with cliff-hanging endings to chapters and a compulsively readable narrative. Why this was Astor's favourite book we will probably never know, but with its historical setting and story based on a young man finding his way in the world, there may have been an element of nostalgic self-identification. Certainly, Dumas's novel was a popular book, but by the 1890s it was some fifty years old and so unlikely to be of interest to many, other than Astor. In embellishing Cliveden, Astor led from the front, for instance designing the garden maze himself in January 1894, and we can assume he was equally involved at the estate office, planning this unique scheme together with Pearson.

Figural carvings on staircases had historical precedents in English architecture, particularly during the Jacobean period, as at Hatfield House in Hertfordshire, but it seems just as likely that Pearson had in mind more recent interiors with ornamental and figural sculpture by the late Augustus Welby Pugin and by William Burges. Pearson knew Burges as a friend and would no doubt have been familiar with Tower House, Burges's own home in Kensington, which was filled with story-telling sculptural decoration. Indeed, when it came to finding an artist-craftsman who could create small-scale figural sculptures of sufficiently high quality, Pearson called on Burges's prime architectural craftsman, Thomas Nicholls (1825/6–96), to carry out the work. Based at his workshop in Lambeth, Nicholls was the senior member of the team at the Astor Estate Office and had the experience and skill to carry out the decorative scheme for the 'musketeers staircase'.

Each character sculpture, about 1½ feet (0.5 metres) in height, is placed on an urn-shaped element and an inverted podium, rising quite high above the stair rail. Approaching the first flight, to the left, one meets d'Artagnan, the central character of the novel, standing in thoughtful pose (figs 38, 39). Opposite is Madame Bonacieux enveloped in her cloak, as she was when the young man discovered her on a secret assignation (fig. 40). On the first landing Aramis, a quiet individual, is engrossed in a book (fig. 41). He is paired with Milady, wearing court dress, the beautiful adventuress who loved and left Athos sometime before the novel opens (fig. 43). Towards the back of the landing Bazin, the valet of Aramis, studies his theology books, while incongruously brushing his master's clothes (fig. 42). On

the second landing the aristocratic Athos appears wearing the uniform of a royal musketeer with a Greek cross on it (fig. 44). His melancholy demeanour and austere manner disguise a secret history with the treacherous Milady, which is revealed as the book unfolds. Completing the group, in a commanding position at the top of the stairs, is Porthos, the burly and loud extrovert of the group, in a swaggering stance with a musket across his shoulder (fig. 45).

Each figure's costume and pose have been carefully considered: did Pearson and Astor confer on the choice of characters and their positions? Of the eight represented, two are absorbed in reading, a signal of Astor's own literary interests. One can imagine visitors taking some pleasure in recognising the characters by their dress or demeanour, and that giving rise to conversation as well as appreciation of such an unusual portrayal of literature. The carver Thomas Nicholls was so fond of the figures that he kept them at his studio and later, when he became ill, in his own bedroom. Reputedly, they were not delivered to the estate office until after his death in March 1896.

Oak panelling covers the entire wall space of the Staircase Hall. Everywhere one looks there are elaborate carved details, such as the naturalistic imagery of birds and leaves and fanciful putti in the spandrels. An ascent to the first floor opens into an arcaded gallery surrounding the staircase. The upper arches are supported by ten solid ebony columns, a spectacular display of this luxury material (fig. 46). Always sourced from exotic locations, ebony was rarely used as an architectural element and more commonly employed in smaller quantities, as in the embellishment of furniture or as parts of musical instruments or chess sets. Indeed, the last usage might well have recommended this material to Astor, for whom chess was a favourite pastime. The shiny black columns positioned around the gallery create a stately rhythm, measuring the space, and their deep black colour contrasts with the warmer-toned mahogany staircase and oak panelling.

Immediately above the ebony columns the literary themes of the decorative scheme are expanded even further with six statuettes sculpted in oak with characters from American novels, each positioned on top of the column capitals, which are additionally animated by grotesque figures peeping out of them. Nicholls carved all these, as he had the ones on the stairs, making the entire Staircase Hall a display of his workmanship. Astor's literary preferences certainly dictated the choice of a selection of well-known American classics, with a focus on the main protagonists in these stories. Hester Prynne (fig. 47) from Nathaniel Hawthorne's *Scarlet Letter* (1850) is denoted by the embroidered

FIGS 39–45 ABOVE AND LEFT
Staircase figures from *The Three Musketeers*
carved by Thomas Nicholls
(top to bottom and left to right):
D'Artagnan (39), Madame Constance Bonacieux (40),
Aramis (41), Bazin (42, above), Milady de Winter (43),
Athos (44) and Porthos (45)

49

letter 'A' on her dress, the sign of her adultery with the Reverend Arthur Dimmesdale, who stands diagonally across the corner of the hall. Her courage in this sad situation stood in contrast to the prim vicar, who lived with his shameful secret. Two character statuettes come from James Fenimore Cooper's *Last of the Mohicans: A Narrative of 1757* (1826), a historical novel set during the Seven Years' War conflict between the French and the British. This book introduced the energetic figure of Natty Bumppo, the trailblazing scout dubbed 'Hawkeye'. Here he is identifiable by his deerskin leggings and long musket, and his backwoods companion, the loyal hunting dog Hector, peering out from behind his legs. Natty is paired with Uncas, the noble savage and 'last Mohican', positioned directly across the hall (fig. 48). He stands with crossed legs in thoughtful pose; sheaves of corn on the spandrels behind him and a beaver on the capital below denote the American setting. Hawkeye and Uncas were so special to Astor that they later appeared on his coat of arms.[56] He seems to have seen an echo of his own grandfather's exploits in the American West in the adventurous characters of the pathfinder and his Indian guide.

Washington Irving's short story, *Rip Van Winkle*, one of the Knickerbocker Tales in *The Sketch Book* (1820), provides the source for two more figures around the Staircase Hall. The elderly bearded Rip, who had slept for twenty years, awoke to find the world around him completely transformed. He looks directly at his rediscovered daughter, Judith Gardenier, now grown up and married. He raises his arm as if to greet her, yet also conscious that he is about to face a new

FIGS 46–8 ABOVE AND RIGHT
The gallery of the Staircase Hall (above left) showing ebony columns and carved figures by Thomas Nicholls, including Hester Prynne (above) and Uncas, the last Mohican (right)

future. The sympathetic Judith turns to gaze across the corner towards him, signalling her acceptance of his return. It is certainly relevant that both Cooper's and Irving's tales are set in upstate New York, an area that Astor was familiar with from his time serving in state government. With Irving there is another close family link to the Astors: John Jacob I commissioned him to write *Astoria* (1836), a hagiographical account of the origins of the family fur-trading empire based in north-western America.

The grouping of the six figures in the Staircase Hall presents a survey of American literature as seen through William Waldorf Astor's eyes. Expanding the literary scope and moving from American to British, a magnificent oak frieze of scenes from Shakespeare's plays surrounds the top of the hall, with each side featuring one of the four dramas, *Henry VIII*, *Othello*, *Antony and Cleopatra* and *Macbeth*. Here Nicholls carved eighty-two characters in high relief to portray some of the best-known and most identifiable passages from these works by the Bard. Astor might well have considered it appropriate to celebrate Shakespeare, as the playwright had an association with the nearby Middle Temple Hall, where the first performance of *Twelfth Night* took place in 1601. In the frieze depicting *Henry VIII* the central figure of the king is garlanded in celebration of his wedding to Anne Boleyn, who stands beside him, while the suspicious Cardinal Wolsey stares at them (fig. 51). The more extended sequence from *Macbeth*

FIGS 49–51 ABOVE AND RIGHT
Sections from the oak frieze in the gallery showing scenes from Shakespeare's *Macbeth* (above and above right) and *Henry VIII* (right), with Cardinal Wolsey, Henry VIII and Anne Boleyn

gives a condensed version of the play, from the point when Banquo's ghost appears at the banquet, through Lady Macbeth's mad scene in the turreted castle staircase, to the fight between Macduff and Macbeth (figs 49, 50). The amount of planning, reading and characterisation achieved here is a testament to the artist-craftsman involved. Later, in 1920, one writer paid tribute to Nicholls commenting that he was a 'craftsman, gone and forgotten, who quite obviously had the rare gift for modelling and a keen perception of grace in figure carving'.[57] All his years of working for Burges reached their culmination at the Astor Estate Office.

The full facts of who created the programme for the friezes are not known and it may be that Pearson's son Frank had some input (he certainly supervised the project). On the other hand, the elder Pearson's concern for the detail of his interiors and Astor's own intimate involvement with literature mean that they probably directed these dramas themselves. The densely populated friezes encourage yet more 'reading' of the decorative scheme, with Astor seeming to ordain that his own love of books should be made visible throughout the building. The comments of J.R. Willis Alexander are pertinent here; when he wrote his account of the house in 1928 at a time when some of the principals were still alive, he described Astor as 'requiring a house which would personify literature in addition to being representative of art, craft and architecture'.[58]

53

THE GREAT ROOM

At the climax of their stately progression up the staircase and into the arcaded gallery visitors entered through a massive carved-mahogany door into the Great Room (fig. 52). This is where Astor held court. The compact, dark and intensely decorated space of the staircase area opens up to the grandeur of the hall filled with light from the two great oriel windows offering views out to the Thames. This 'palatial apartment' runs the full length of the building, over 70 feet (21 metres) at its longest, with its open timber hammer-beam roof consciously rising to the challenge of emulating medieval and Tudor precedents (fig. 53). Pearson knew well how to handle such a feature, not least because his role as surveyor at Westminster Abbey gave him responsibility for the greatest hammer-beam roof in the country at Westminster Hall. He took this grand traditional form into another realm with his use of Spanish mahogany wood and the sophisticated decorative detailing in the spirit of the Gothic and Renaissance eras.

Fluted mahogany pilasters divide the wall into bays of pencil-cedar panelling (some of which was replaced during post-war restoration). A particular choice, this reddish wood, in reality derived from the juniper tree, attracts close scrutiny of its fine delicate graining. The tree itself, noted for its scent, is prevalent in eastern America, another factor that may have recommended it to Astor. The

FIGS 52–3 BELOW AND RIGHT
The Great Room looking west (below) and east (right) with hammer-beam ceiling

entire space has wood panelling except for blank empty sections at each end of the hammer-beam roof. These bare undecorated areas of plain stonework seem incongruous amid the rich effects elsewhere in the room, but they are a feature of Tudor and neo-Tudor halls and here serve to emphasise the intensity of surface detailing throughout the room. At each end of the Great Room, set within matching arched spaces, rose fireplaces, only one of which, on the eastern side, now survives *in situ*; for the one on the western side, see Pearson's drawing (fig. 54). These are flanked by wide recessed inglenooks backed with stained-glass windows and elaborately carved benches, where those waiting for an audience with Astor might sit enjoying the decoration surrounding them. The wood carving was carried out by Nathaniel Hitch, whose talent shines out in all aspects of his work, but is especially visible in the carved bench ends, where powerfully modelled forms, such as a writhing mermaid and a roaring lion (fig. 55), burst out from the confines of their designated role as arm rests.

The one chimneypiece that remains is another key element in the decorative scheme (fig. 56).[59] Modelled freely on French Renaissance precedents, it is fully carved in pencil cedar with two pairs of caryatid-type figures, one male and one female. Between them a narrow, upright window appears unexpectedly on each side, providing light as well as views out to Milford Lane. Hitch's lively carving contains many felicitous details, including a lobster above one of the caryatids (perhaps because Astor was a noted gourmet). On the upper portion of the chimneypiece paired columns support an elaborate superstructure that contains a niched, arched compartment, specially designed to display a statuette. Astor's collection included several Renaissance bronzes and small marbles, one of which might have once stood here; today, another figure may fill this position.[60] Still original to the room are the baronial, gilded wrought-iron chandeliers, with vigorous modelled branches that were probably designed by Frith,[61] and the polished hardwood floor arranged in hexagonal and octagonal patterns.

As one looks further upwards, to the supporting brackets under the roof, twelve carved statuettes gaze down from elaborate traceried canopies (fig. 57). Much like saints on a Gothic cathedral, they are in fact characters from another novel Astor knew well, Sir Walter Scott's *Ivanhoe* (1819). Once the statues were in position, high up in the dark upper reaches of the room, Astor, due to his short-sightedness, requested that they be gilded, something that Hitch, who carried out all the carving for the Great Room, objected to ('because a rich man had very poor eyesight'[62]) – but gilded they were.

Hitch, as we have seen, did much of the exterior carving; here in the Great Room he carried on in the manner of Nicholls by incorporating individually

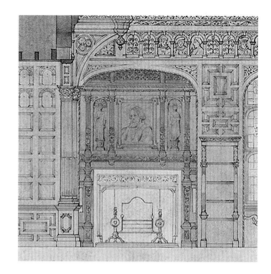

Fig. 55 ABOVE
Bench end in the Great Room carved by Nathaniel Hitch

Fig. 54 TOP
Detail of Pearson's drawing of the Great Room (fig. 15) showing the fireplace

Fig. 56 RIGHT
Fireplace at the east end of the Great Room

Part of the Great Room ceiling (left)
showing statuettes from *Ivanhoe* carved
by Nathaniel Hitch, with details of
Ivanhoe (top) and Maid Marian (above)

characterised figures from literature into the decorative scheme. Scott's *Ivanhoe*, one of the Waverley novels, was a great popular success in its day. Set in twelfth-century England, it focuses on the crusader, Richard Coeur de Lion, King of England, who returns from captivity in Austria with the help of Ivanhoe and proceeds to overturn his brother John, who has usurped the throne. The story has all the ingredients of a historical romance with thwarted lovers and great set pieces such as royal jousts. A sprawling cast of characters includes Ivanhoe (fig. 58), Rowena, the jester Wamba, the swineherd Gurth, Front de Boeuf, Sir Brian de Bois-Guilbert (the Templar), Robin Hood, Maid Marian (fig. 59) and Friar Tuck. Their colourful exploits fed into a fictionalised account of English history, a mixture that appealed greatly to Astor. In this Great Room, modelled on early English architectural precedents, Scott's novel, set in the medieval era, provides chronologically apt material for the decorative scheme.

The literary themes merged with history in one of the most noteworthy aspects of the interior. Around the top portion of the Great Room a frieze of fifty individual portrait heads (several now gone), modelled in low relief, forms a hall of fame attracting the observer's eye. The heads can be seen in the architectural drawings of 1892 and were certainly part of Pearson's original design (fig. 60). This room fulfilled Astor's request for a building that could be read as well as used. The heads, each carved in low relief by Hitch and gilded, show groups of historical and fictional individuals arranged in no particular order and resulting in some tantalising, if meaningless, juxtapositions. Over the central doorway, the prime position in the whole room, one finds a philosopher, a French-born consort and eventual widow of Charles I, and a Renaissance writer on statecraft and power politics: Voltaire (fig. 61), Queen Henrietta Maria and Machiavelli. Another grouping comprises Anne Boleyn (emphatically labelled 'Qn. Anne Boleyn' and foreshadowing Astor's later purchase of her home, Hever Castle), Columbus, and Jessica, Shylock's daughter from *The Merchant of Venice* (fig. 62).

There is no need to look for connections because the whole accumulation is entirely personal to Astor. His taste for tragic heroines, fallen queens and damsels in distress is evident in the predominance of female literary characters from Shakespeare and Tennyson: Juliet, Desdemona, Ophelia, Cordelia, Fair Rosamund, Elaine, Queen Guinevere, Lady Clara Vere de Vere and the Lady of Shalott. Not surprisingly, given Astor's own novels set in the Renaissance, this era is well represented by Dante, Galileo, Gabrielle d'Este, Lorenzo de' Medici and the artists Michelangelo and Raphael. Even explorers feature: Columbus, Marco Polo and Captain Cook. There are some individuals whom only Astor could love: John Ericsson, a Swedish-American naval engineer who

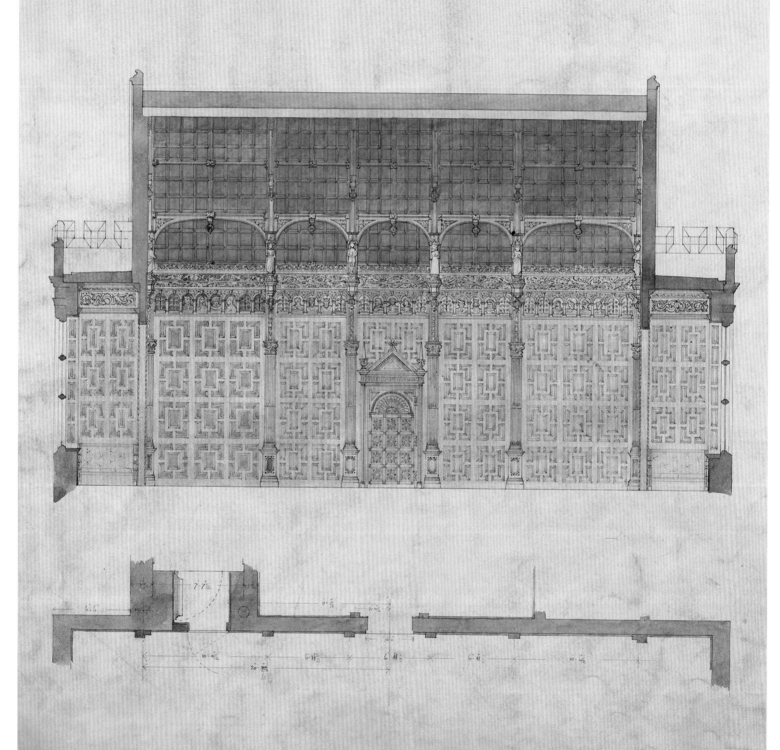

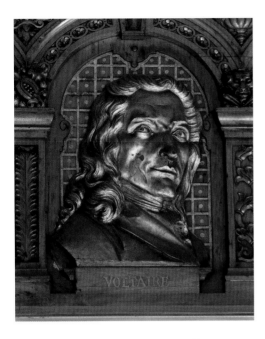

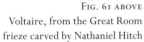

FIG. 61 ABOVE
Voltaire, from the Great Room
frieze carved by Nathaniel Hitch

FIG. 61 ABOVE
Voltaire, from the Great Room
frieze carved by Nathaniel Hitch

FIG. 62 ABOVE RIGHT
Anne Boleyn, Columbus and Jessica
from the Great Room frieze

FIG. 60 LEFT
John Loughborough Pearson,
'Astor Estate Office, The Great Room',
north section and plan, signed and
dated June 1892, sepia and coloured
washes (RIBA Library Drawings
and Archives Collection)

died in 1889, and Otto von Bismarck (fig. 63), the former Prussian Chancellor, who seems to be the sole example of someone still living in 1894. Astor, with his taste for military history, would have admired the exploits of 'The Iron Chancellor' in Europe, though Bismarck was out of favour at this time, having resigned from high office.

In 'reading' this decorative scheme, we find no obvious narrative or iconography; each individual is here because they belonged to Astor's own personal pantheon. The sheer amount of effort that must have gone into sourcing accurate representations, in order to create a portrait that convinced, is extraordinary, and Hitch's success is a vivid testimony to the uniqueness of the programme. In no other contemporary interior can one find such a lavish and historically detailed plan; it only happened because a man obsessed with literature and the past had the wish and the means to fulfil his fantastic imaginings.

In the Great Room the most beautiful element of the decorative scheme, the elaborate main doorway, acts as a key focal point with its silver-gilt relief figures (fig. 65). The sculptural embellishment showing nine Arthurian heroines was designed and executed by George Frampton (1860–1928). On Pearson's drawing of June 1892, the door is divided into nine compartments (fig. 60), though not at this point with figural decoration. Perhaps in the course of planning, and with the advice of Frith and Nathaniel Hitch, the leading decorator of this Great Room, it was decided to seek out an artist who could make a distinctive

contribution. Frampton, by far the youngest contributor to the project, did not have a track record of working with Pearson before. It seems likely that Frith recommended his former star student from the modelling classes at the South London School of Technical Art in Lambeth. Frampton's skills were such that he moved on to study at the Royal Academy Schools and in Paris. In the 1880s he actively pursued a career as an ornamental sculptor for architectural interiors and exteriors. Considering himself an 'art worker', rather than just a sculptor, Frampton joined the Art Workers' Guild and took advantage of periodicals such as *The Studio*, then newly formed, to advance his career. He worked in various genres and media and also designed medals and jewellery, learning to elaborate his surfaces with differing and contrasting materials and colours. By the early 1890s he was a regular exhibitor at the Royal Academy, with individual sculptures in a highly personal Symbolist style and often showing enigmatic female figures. One of these, *Mysteriarch* (1892; Walker Art Gallery, Liverpool), appeared at public exhibition at the same time as the Astor commission; it shows that, however much Frampton wished to be seen as a craftsman, he also had clear ambitions to be a 'fine' artist. In this he was unique among the collaborators at the estate office.

In recruiting an up-and-coming, highly ambitious artist and assigning him a prominent position, Pearson reinforced Frampton's privileged status. In the architect's early drawing the door is not decorated with figural panels. As completed, it shows nine Arthurian women (fig. 65; from top to bottom and

FIG. 65
The main Great Room door
with panel figures in relief
by George Frampton

left to right): the Lady of the Isle of Avelyon, Elaine (the Fair Maid of Astolat), the Lady of the Lake, Morgan le Fay, Guinevere, La Beale Isoude, Lyonors, Enid and lastly Alis la Beale Pilgrim. Was the subject matter left to Frampton's choice or did it grow out of Astor's fascination with the romantic heroines of literature? Guinevere also appears in Hitch's frieze of famous heads surrounding the upper reaches of the room. Yet this young sculptor had already shown his own obsession with female subjects in his sculpture and decorative work.

Frampton almost certainly planned his own detailed programme, for he was concerned enough that observers would know who was who to inscribe the names of the characters on each panel. Several sources served him, chiefly Thomas Malory's *Morte d'Arthur*, a fifteenth-century cycle of Arthurian legends, as well as the more recent poetical works of Alfred Tennyson, especially *The Idylls of the King* with the first volume (1859) containing the poems, 'Enid', 'Vivien', 'Elaine' and 'Guinevere'. Malory's focus is squarely on the male protagonists of the Arthurian saga; Tennyson recounts the legends with a greater emphasis on the female characters interacting with men in the main tale of King Arthur and his Queen Guinevere, the ruin of his kingdom and his eventual death. The other leading characters are Lancelot, with whom Guinevere runs away, and his former love Elaine. By the 1890s the blended identities of the Arthurian women were well known through their appearance as the subject matter of Pre-Raphaelite works of art, such as the Oxford Union murals of 1857, and of Pre-Raphaelite poetry, not to mention the popularity of such themes in the work of their followers. Frampton belonged to this tradition, but he brought his own personal scholarly emphasis by depicting some of the more unusual characters, such as Alis La Beale Pilgrim, who makes only a passing appearance in Malory and none at all in Tennyson. The artist's choice of archaising spelling (such as 'beale' for 'belle') for the characters also suggests a desire to get back to the medieval roots of the saga.

Frampton went even further than Tennyson in his engagement with the women of the Arthurian tales. The whole door is a tribute to them, elevating these medieval ladies to centre stage. Each woman is placed within a decorated arched enclosure and is characterised with appropriate accessories to give any viewer familiar with the tale some clues to their identity. The central focus is appropriately on the main character, Queen Guinevere (fig. 71), her royal status signalled by a relaxed demeanour and placement on a throne edged with her name and decorated with images of knights. Her position and characterisation immediately convey the sense that the whole saga hinges on her exploits with King Arthur and Lancelot. This is the only panel of the group that Frampton signed with his initial and surname (several others are initialled simply 'G.F.'). To one side of Guinevere a semi-nude Morgan le Fay, sorceress sister of King Arthur, plays her harp as if casting a magical spell (fig. 70). On the other side La Beale Isoude also plays a musical instrument, a portable organ, as she gazes forlornly out of a window (fig. 72), the cause of her sadness being an arranged marriage with King Mark, despite her love for Sir Tristram. In the upper row of figures is first the Lady of the Isle of Avelyon with a sword (fig. 67), followed by Elaine, the Fair Maid of Astolat (fig. 68), who guards the sacred shield of Sir Lancelot. Her unrequited love for that knight and his liaison with Guinevere lead to Elaine's eventual death from a broken heart. The third character on this row is the Lady of the Lake, a supernatural creature who gives Arthur the sword of Excalibur, which she is seen holding in its elaborate scabbard (fig. 69). The lowest row shows three minor players in the legend: Lyonors (fig. 73), sitting dejectedly, since she was held prisoner in her castle until saved by Sir Gareth; the faithful Enid (fig. 74), married to Geraint, whose suspicions she overcame by her devotion; and finally the little-known Alis la Beale Pilgrim (fig. 75), kinswoman to Sir Lancelot and wife to the slaughtered knight Sir Alisaunder. She unfurls a scroll on her knees, perhaps in an allusion to the writing and reading of the Arthurian saga itself.

Throughout all these images of women there is an air of melancholy, for some met tragic ends, others were merely sad, but the emotion is clear and perfectly in keeping with William Waldorf Astor's own romantic temperament. One tiny touch of humour can be found: in the middle of the fan-like arched compartment over the door itself sits a cheeky putto (fig. 66), legs splayed, crossing his arms and with an expression on his face that might just be read as an ironic comment on the forlorn ladies of the Arthurian court. This little fellow, unlikely to be by Frampton, is more in keeping with the earthy sensibility of Nathaniel Hitch.

Originally modelled in plaster, Frampton's panels were cast in bronze with silver gilt applied. The effect is jewel-like and delicate. The challenge for the artist was to create a work of decorative art worthy of the key position in the room. It had to act in concert with the other sculptural decoration – the Ivanhoe figures and the frieze of famous heads. Yet it had to avoid being overpowered by the vast wood-panelled space topped by the hammer-beam ceiling. The result is the most magnificent feature of the building, a remarkable tour de force of decorative splendour, its silver-gilt surface sparkling in bright light and glistening in the shadows when the atmosphere is more sombre. Incomparably delicate in its low relief modelling, it draws one closer to study the individual panels. The figure of Guinevere wears a dress with precise Celtic patterns on it; wavy lines behind

FIG. 66 ABOVE
Putto above the Great Room door panels

FIGS 67–75 RIGHT
Figural panels on the Great Room door

Top row: Lady of the Isle of Avelyon (67); Elaine, the Fair Maid of Astolat (68); the Lady of the Lake (69)
Middle row: Morgan le Fay (70); Guinevere (71); La Beale Isoude (72)
Bottom row: Lyonors (73); Enid (74); Alis la Beale Pilgrim (75)

FIGS 76–8 LEFT AND ABOVE
Sunrise, stained-glass window by
Clayton and Bell at the eastern
end of the Great Room, and
details (above)

the Lady of the Lake suggest water. Frampton believed that 'the charm of low relief is its delicate lights and shades, and the losing and finding of the design'.[63] In these panels the elusive elements of the backgrounds or detailing reward close scrutiny, yet so precise and fine is some of the imagery in the panels that it was destined to remain only hinted at after the casting process.

Why Frampton worked these panels up in such detail can be partly explained by the fact that he intended to create independent works of art from some of them. Once the decoration for the door was installed, he exhibited some of the panels at the Royal Academy in 1896 with the title: 'Seven heroines out of "Mort d'Arthur" – panel for a door.' In the next few years he extracted several separate reliefs, including Alis La Beale Pilgrim, as stand-alone works of art for sale. It was common practice for sculptors to profit from public commissions by recycling reduced versions, but the commission at the estate office was for a notoriously private client and one wonders how Astor would have felt about this reuse of his 'ladies'. There is also an account that some of Frampton's work displeased J.L. Pearson's son Frank,[64] who was supervising the project; apparently, the sculptor grudgingly made some changes but these did not entirely satisfy Frank. What might have brought further irritation was the fact that Frampton signed his name on the main panel of the door and initialled others. To the architect this gesture must have seemed like an assertion of the status of the individual artist rather than being an anonymous collaborator in his team. Frampton clearly came from a different generation to Nicholls, Frith and Hitch, and had his eye on his future career.

The elaborate stained-glass windows in the inglenooks are the most colourful ingredients of the Great Room's decorative scheme (figs 76–82). Here again, Pearson called on long-time collaborators: John Robert Clayton (1827–1913), the principal designer, and Alfred Bell (1832–95), who had also produced the skylight window at the top of the Staircase Hall. This well-established firm dated from the 1850s. They had a long association with George Gilbert Scott and participated in several projects by Pearson, most recently at St Augustine's, Kilburn, and Truro Cathedral. They ran a big workshop and were equally adept at mosaic and mural decoration. For the estate office Clayton and Bell produced two dramatic windows that were very much one-offs. At the time ecclesiastical glass commissions far outweighed ones for domestic interiors. Morris and Company produced glass for homes, some based on Arthurian themes; and William Burges delighted in stained glass especially at his own home, Tower House in Kensington, where Chaucerian themes and medievalising allegories prevailed. In general, interior stained glass featured heraldic motifs; indeed,

Pearson's original drawing of the room shows something very like that in place. But, as with the commission executed by Frampton, discussions had moved on, either through Pearson's own suggestions or Astor's comments on the drawings. The resulting windows are striking additions to the Great Room.

Clayton and Bell's firm produced two glorious landscapes in stained glass, conceived as a pair, at opposite ends of the Great Room. The one at the eastern end shows a sunrise and the matching one to the west depicts an evening scene. These views seem to fly in the face of the then current convention that stained glass should not resemble an easel painting, nor should it call attention to itself as an isolated element in the decorative scheme of a room. At nearly 11 feet (3.4 metres) high and 9 feet (2.7 metres) wide, the landscape windows are prominent and powerful elements in the design of the room. Treating the whole area of the glass and mullions as one view, rather than addressing each compartment separately, results in an artwork that is, quite literally, a picture window. As they can be read from a distance, any visitor to the Great Room can see them from the entrance door. Yet the windows are also filled with much specific information – details of the people, the landscape, the architecture, the boats and so on – so that anyone seated near by (in what is, after all, a sitting area with benches) can enjoy the spectacle close-up, reading all the minute detail of plants and other images painted onto the glass in the foreground.

Sunrise shows mountains descending down to a great river with a fairy-tale turreted castle sited on a promontory (fig. 77). A sailboat laden with logs makes its way along the river. A telling detailing is the red flag with white cross, for this identifies the setting as Switzerland (fig. 78). A link with the Astor family's past may well have suggested the subject: John Jacob Astor I, the founder of the dynasty, had once possessed a villa on Lake Geneva. Was the Swiss landscape yet another act of filial piety, making reference to a location that had entered into family mythology as a beautiful distant place, far removed from the urban lives that the Astors led in New York and London?

The figures in *Sunrise* provide some slight narrative, as a hearty swain, carrying his scythe and heading up to the hills, gazes at a young woman going to market. Yet these figures might be intended simply as rustics enacting daily activities of country life. The landscape prospect depicts the beginning of the day; later, in *Sunset* a different view features a distant town, from where peasant milkmaids and their cows return home against a backdrop of high mountains and a sky layered with the hot pinks, reds and oranges of sunset (fig. 79). Again, might there be a storyline, as a solitary pilgrim heads down the road past two country

FIGS 79–81 ABOVE AND RIGHT
Sunset, stained-glass window by Clayton and Bell at the western end of the Great Room, and details (above)

girls (fig. 80)? Nothing is spelled out. We see an idyllic view of a distant country where nature and people are in harmony. The well-ordered landscape, cultivated with grapevines, co-exists with the wild mountain range and streaming waterfalls (fig. 82). Individuals attend to their country chores, with only the pilgrim suggesting a life and aspiration going beyond this particular place. With no known documentation about the commission in the literature on Clayton and Bell, we can only speculate on how it came about. But again one senses that Astor led the way. Did this ex-New Yorker recall recent lavish interiors in his home city, such as that of William Henry Vanderbilt, which contained elaborate pictorial stained glass by the artist John La Farge dating from the early 1880s, or indeed interiors with glass by Louis Comfort Tiffany?[65] Was Astor intending to rival such 'Gilded Age' decoration in his new London interior? It seems likely, as there was little precedent for such predominant stained glass in English secular buildings. What is certain is that these two windows offer a spectacular display of coloured glass characterised by brilliant luminosity and a variety of surface effects, marking an advance on the use of stained glass in Britain in the 1890s. *Sunrise* and *Sunset* are as far away from the medieval ideal of Morris and Co. as can be imagined and compare directly with the 'art glass' of American Gilded Age interiors.

HOW DID THE GREAT ROOM FUNCTION FOR ASTOR?

As a public and private area, this room epitomised Astor's family, his business pursuits and his own personal interests (fig. 83). Directly in the centre of the vast space, he sat enthroned at an impressive desk, supported by sphinx-like figures. From this position he could admire the beautiful door with Frampton's silver-gilt panels or, if facing in the other direction, enjoy a wide view of the Thames, surrounded by an array of elaborately decorated antique furniture acquired during his years in Italy. He also commissioned specific new pieces, such as the desk and cabinets designed by John Dibblee Crace.[66]

One curious incident concerning the furnishing of the Great Room reveals Astor's social and aesthetic insecurities. He asked his editor Harry Cust (a member of the aristocratic Brownlow family) to visit and posed a question: 'Now, Mr Cust, you are a man of unerring taste, I want you to tell me what is the matter with this room. I feel there is something wrong, but I can't quite make out what it is.' Cust had a ready answer: 'Well that's easy enough to see. You've got a cedar wood room, with ebony furniture, looking like blobs of ink all over the floor.' Astor quickly recovered from this criticism: 'Of course, of course, I was quite sure that you would at once spot the defect.'[67] The aesthetic gaffe of mixing ebony and cedar in one room may explain why Astor commissioned new pieces from Crace.

FIG. 82 ABOVE
Sunset, detail

FIG. 83 RIGHT
The Great Room in Astor's time, late 1890s, from the sale catalogue, 1920 (Centre for Buckinghamshire Studies)

The key theme in the Great Room, as it was originally arranged in the 1890s, was a celebration of Astor's family dynasty. Portraits of his immediate forebears were prominently displayed, with that of the young John Jacob Astor I (c.1794; private collection) by the expatriate American artist, Gilbert Stuart, set into the panelling above the western fireplace (fig. 54). It was important to Astor to pay tribute to his great-grandfather John Jacob, 'The Landlord of New York', who is also referred to in the inscription on the portico, as the founder of the dynasty. But the continuing lineage also mattered. Flanking each side of the central door were portraits of his grandfather, William Backhouse Astor (1792–1875), by George Augustus Baker (1872) and of his father, John Jacob III (1822–90), by the Spanish artist, Raimundo Madrazo (1884). Reinforcing the line of succession, Astor's own portrait by Hubert von Herkomer (fig. 84) joined the group hanging here. Herkomer's reputation with American clients was such that Astor felt comfortable with him. This portrait gives a sympathetic and approachable impression of the sitter, somewhat at odds with his public reputation but perhaps truer to the man himself than hearsay in the press.

Throughout the 1890s and later, key decisions on the Astor Estate – the planning and building of great hotels, such as the Netherland, and apartment blocks in New York City – received his approval in this room. Astor's environment contained comfortable sofas and tiger-skin rugs, as can also be seen in old photographs. It was not an office per se, but a place that reflected Astor's interests. To one side a concealed panel led to a steel door opening into the strongroom (no longer extant), where money and securities were stockpiled in safety. Despite his reputation as a strange character, Astor often met with his friends and family in the Great Room. He was particularly close to John, his younger son, who even late in life recalled often having lunch or dinner with his father there. Astor liked nothing better than discussions with John about military history in this room where the decorative scheme, such as the portrait of Bismarck in the frieze of famous heads, prompted debate.

THE LIBRARY

Although several built-in bookcases can be seen in the Great Room, for Astor, the zealous bibliophile, the adjoining Library contained the main part of the collection he kept at the estate office (figs 85–9). This gathering was only a fraction of his wide-ranging collection, which featured many treasures, especially rare illuminated medieval manuscripts.[69] Building libraries was something of a family preoccupation; his great-grandfather bequeathed money at his death in 1848 for the founding of a free public library in New York City, which eventually became one of the cornerstones of the great New York Public Library. Astor's

Fig. 84 ABOVE
Hubert von Herkomer, *William Waldorf Astor*, 1898, oil on canvas (National Trust Images, Cliveden: The Astor Collection)

Fig. 85 ABOVE RIGHT
John Loughborough Pearson, 'The Library at the Astor Estate Office' (detail), sepia pen and coloured washes (RIBA Library Drawings and Archives Collection)

Fig. 86 RIGHT
The Library, showing the wall and door opposite the window

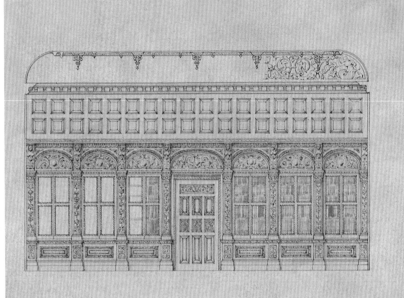

own library focused on manuscripts and historical material associated with great individuals. His ardent involvement with the past expressed itself in a collection of letters written by renowned figures like Samuel Pepys, Lord Byron, Charles Dickens and many others, and he would read, handle and study these during his solitary hours in the library. This passion to experience the reality of the past also lay behind the frieze of famous people in the Great Room. To him the study of celebrated achievers provided role models for life. Napoleon loomed large in his pantheon.

Designed as a wholly private retreat, the Library in the estate office had its door from the Great Room cunningly disguised in the panelling. Pearson provided a specific plan for the whole room, as seen in his drawing (fig. 85), which shows a level of refined elaboration in every element of the design. The superb moulded plasterwork ceiling (now gone) was a tour de force, and with that in place the room looked like a Jacobean or Tudor chamber. Handsome woodwork included polished mahogany flooring and panelling in satinwood.[70] The room is not large, and in Astor's time the daylight was partially blocked by the nearby Middle Temple Library, so the choice of satinwood was practical as well as attractive, as it could be polished to a very glossy finish to reflect light. Satinwood, fashionable in the late eighteenth century, had links with Georgian furniture and the age of Robert Adam, epitomising a new lightness in design. This association suited the historically minded Astor, as did the idea of using different types of wood in each room, almost as if he sought to produce a catalogue of luxury woods, many associated with the Americas. Pearson himself also exploited natural materials for the colouristic qualities, so the red mahogany, pencil cedar, pale satinwoods and dark Cuban sabicu (in Astor's bedroom, see below) provided a means to achieve surface richness and texture.

Frith had charge of the Library's decorative scheme, much as Nicholls had carried out the Staircase Hall designs and Hitch had responsibility for the Great Room. In keeping with the refinements that satinwood encouraged, due to its dense grain and light colour, the very low relief carving is exceptionally delicate, quite the opposite of Hitch's vigorous style. Frith's skill is amply evident in a decorative scheme loosely based on the arts and sciences. A set of six bookcases, with the door at the centre, is ranged along the wall opposite the window, forming seven bays across the room. Applied pilasters dividing each bay are capped by putto herm figures, some holding musical instruments and others with scientific devices. Across the top of each bay is an arched compartment filled with sinuous carved plant forms that merge into fantastical animals and a female head. The door and its surrounding pilasters contain yet more elegant

FIG. 87 ABOVE
The Library door to the gallery, with carving by William Silver Frith

FIG. 88 RIGHT
The Library in Astor's time, late 1890s, showing carved fireplace and overmantel by William Silver Frith (photograph © Country Life Picture Library)

carving (fig. 87). Six cupid figures in relief are arrayed on the door in imitation of Renaissance grotesquerie. Fortunately, all this carving remains, although due to bombing during the war, the ceiling was lost and restorations were necessary.

Originally, the main focus in the Library was Frith's monumental fireplace in white marble, a massive addition that necessitated steel joists in the wall for reinforcement. Again, due to the reconstruction of this part of the building (see below, pp. 87–9), the fireplace had to be removed,[71] but it still exists in storage and its appearance *in situ* is known from old photographs. The lower portion harks back to neoclassical precedents with two semi-nude female caryatids. The upper section, with two sets of columns, one pair with twisting vines around it, frames an original confection: a marble panel filled with little putti, each holding a miniature shield bearing the name of one of Astor's forebears, almost like a family tree in marble and as bizarre as it is charming. Pearson's architectural drawing had offered two possible versions of the chimneypiece, the second revealed by lifting a flap on the drawing. But his design was quite standard with a heraldic shield in the centre, while Frith came up with something much more interesting. The putti are clearly related to the androgynous figures on the bronze lamp standards outside the house. But there is no getting away from the fact that this very odd chimneypiece presents a decidedly eccentric celebration of Astor's ancestry.

Here in his inner sanctum Astor gathered around himself some of his more unusual collectors' items (fig. 89): a medieval-style reading stand, a spinning wheel and historical musical instruments. His rare chess sets tell of his fascination with that game, a model for life in his view:

> The exercise of chess proves that in all things, concentration is the
> secret of success; that time is decisive; that to one battled by the world,
> attack may be the best defence; that a broad margin must be left for
> the Unforeseen which is continually present in our larger game; that
> in life's arena, as on the board, an astute and dramatic move works
> transformation. In all ages, men of achievement have possessed the art
> to convert their pawns to pieces.[72]

This eccentric 'cabinet of curiosities' served as Astor's sanctuary, a place where he could investigate genealogy in his quest for lineage to a noble Spanish family, compose his short stories (regularly published in his own deluxe title, *The Pall Mall Magazine*), study the occult, pore over his manuscript collection and pursue his passion for chess. Most bizarrely, his permanent companion was a life-size *poupée* mannequin holding a mandolin and looking rather creepily lifelike.

Fig. 89
The Library, c.1920, with mannequin holding
a mandolin (photograph © Country Life
Picture Library)

THE BEDROOM

The final room of the house, which is no longer extant, provides a major clue as to how this unique building eventually served its patron. Integral to the architectural plans were a modestly sized bedroom for Astor, significantly placed directly next to the strongroom. It was destroyed during the war and we only know its appearance from archival photographs (fig. 90) and descriptions, but it seems to have been as unusual as the rest of the house. Nathaniel Hitch produced a wide floral frieze to encircle the oval shape formed by the sunken roof above. Both were gilded, making this room like an unearthly golden dream, and the fact that Astor slept in a historical artefact, an elaborate French-style four-poster bed, reputedly of the period of Louis XVI, only enhanced the strange fantastical atmosphere. The panelling in another rare tropical hardwood, the dark Cuban sabicu, added to the sense of luxurious enclosure.

THE DECORATIVE SCHEME

It is important to emphasise that, for all Astor's input in terms of specific literary and symbolic references, Pearson controlled the decorative scheme. The 'look' of the interior of Two Temple Place displays the architect's signature style refined to its essence. Any experience of his best architecture, as at St Augustine's, Kilburn, for example, reveals his talent for creating interiors with powerfully expressed and completely unified surface embellishment. Sculpture, ranging from the finest low-relief carving to bold individual figural statuettes, always plays a major role in these interiors; indeed, at the estate office the sculptural decoration conveys the meaning, as well as the beauty, of the scheme. Here Pearson had the luxury of allowing sumptuous and unusual wood types and exotic marbles to prevail, so that the entire design has an all-encompassing magnificence, absolutely suited to its patron.

ASTOR AT THE ESTATE OFFICE: 'THERE, AT LEAST, I AM SAFE'

Why did Astor have a bedroom at the office? This goes to the heart of the matter, but we must backtrack to consider his life at this point. The building was well under way by 1893. No. 18 Carlton House Terrace served as his public base, where the family lived and where he entertained in grand style. Here he also engaged the Pearsons, father and son, to carry out extensive redecorations, which proceeded in tandem with Temple Place. Meanwhile, the refurbishments continued at his country residence, Cliveden in Buckinghamshire (where he famously installed the entire stone balustrade he purchased from the Villa Borghese in Rome). According to one account, Astor was deeply involved with all the plans for the estate office, an occupation that gave him great pleasure. But in the midst of these preparations a tragedy befell the family: in December 1894 his American wife Mary died, aged only thirty-six. She had never fully recovered from the birth of their fourth child in 1889 and, despite being much liked in London, she missed her homeland. This huge upheaval hit Astor hard. Mary's body had to be transported back to New York for burial (something she may herself have wished). Astor had to face the fact that he was now a widower with a young family, the children aged between five and fifteen years, with the youngest, Gwendolyn, suffering from consumption. His personality is often subjected to criticism, and he was certainly an odd and isolated man, but the loss of his wife accentuated his more reclusive tendencies. Astor was said to be a distant and unfeeling father, but one photograph showing him with his children reveals a man who seems at one with his family, with a benign expression far removed from the aloof image so often presented (fig. 91).

Thoughts of mortality preoccupied Astor. In September 1896, when in his late forties, he wrote a short statement on estate office notepaper setting out the arrangements for his death (fig. 92) – a funeral at St George's, Hanover Square, or at Carlton House Terrace and 'my body to be conveyed thence to a London Crematory & wholly destroyed'.[73] In re-evaluating his life, he arrived at certain key decisions. He sought British citizenship by naturalisation (which came through in 1899) and vowed never to live in the United States again, declaring it 'unfit for a gentleman to live in'.[74] He renounced his American citizenship,

Fig. 91
William Waldorf Astor and his children, Pauline (left), John (standing left), Waldorf (standing right) and Gwendolyn (right), c.1898 (photograph from Gavin Astor, *The Astor Family*, London 1970)

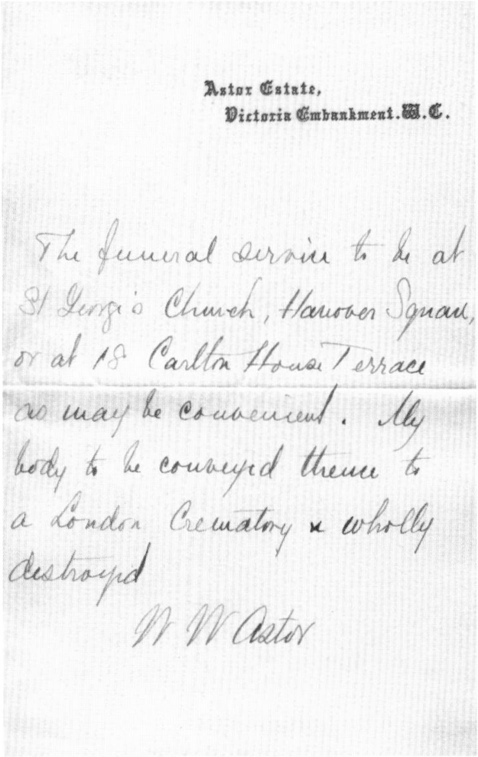

Astor Estate,
Victoria Embankment. W.C.

The funeral service to be at St George's Church, Hanover Square, or at 18 Carlton House Terrace as may be convenient. My body to be conveyed thence to a London Crematory & wholly destroyed

W W Astor

FIG. 92
Astor's letter with his funeral wishes,
1896 (private collection)

making a complete break with his past. Newspapers picked up on the story. The *Manchester Guardian* on 5 January 1900 commented that he had 'finally severed all connection with the land of his birth … and had no intention of living in America again'.[75] Ever after, this gesture nagged at his compatriots, often resulting in biting criticism or sometimes more mellow observations, such as Albert Lavering's chromolithograph cartoon in 1905 for *Life* magazine, showing the great man travelling on the cruise liner, H.M.S.S. Britannia, as 'William Waldorf Astor, Englishman' (fig. 93).[76]

Indeed, Astor's first years in residence in London had confirmed his affinity for this country. It was no secret that he desired a title. He bestowed money on the Conservative party, paid vast sums to charities and pursued friendship with the Prince of Wales and his circle, even buying horses so he could join in with the racing set. Talk in the newspapers was that Astor expected to be raised to the peerage as Lord Cliveden of Taplow but his sometimes odd behaviour and gauche approach to social situations spoiled his chances. In 1898, when the *Daily Mail* reported that a massive section of a redwood tree trunk from California had arrived at Cliveden (to serve as a table at one of Astor's dinner parties), he sued the paper for libel, claiming that they 'held him up to ridicule and contempt'.[77] Clearly, he lacked a sense of humour. Such awkward episodes were nothing compared to the occasion in 1900 when Astor snubbed Sir Berkeley Milne, a friend of the Prince of Wales, who dared to come to a party at 18 Carlton House Terrace without an invitation. Excessively punctilious about correct form, Astor refused him entry. The episode blew up in his face, as it hit the newspapers, and seemingly cost him an early ennoblement after Edward VII acceded to the throne in 1901 (Astor had to wait nearly fifteen years before he finally joined the English nobility).

Well under way by the time of his wife's death in December 1894, the estate office was ready for occupancy the next year and then it truly became Astor's retreat from the world. He had been deeply involved in the early stages, but as one journalist recounted in November 1895:

> When the Astor Estate Office, on the Thames Embankment, which is now approaching completion, was commenced, Mr Astor took the greatest interest in all the details. But since the death of his wife he has been comparatively indifferent to the progress made with the work. It is, however, certain that the building will attract a good deal of attention, both on account of the richness of its ornamentation, and also because of the pains which have been obviously taken in carrying out the plans of the architect.[78]

LIFE
COPYRIGHT, 1905

ALBERT
LEVERING

H.M. S.S. BRITANNIA LIFE PRESERVER

WILLIAM WALDORF
ASTOR, Englishman

He was so busy writing his stories that it was harder to obtain an audience with him than the prime minister of Great Britain

Interestingly, this comment refers both to Astor's keen interest in the details of the project and to Pearson's exacting and high standards. Due to Astor's secretive nature, not much information seeped out about the project, but the activities on site attracted journalistic interest in both British and American newspapers. One writer commented that he has 'built for himself an office, a gem of a building on the Embankment … It sports a splendid gilded weathervane.'[79] As a new feature of the London scene, it drew comment in the press both at home and abroad. In April 1896 *The New York World* came to call, noticing the 'hideous griffins' and gargoyles decorating the exterior; within, a 'gigantic gold laced porter' guarded a ground floor filled with an army of clerks. The reporter sought an interview with Astor, who was sequestered in his private office, where he was so busy writing his stories that it was harder to obtain an audience with him than the prime minister of Great Britain.[80] Personal publicity Astor resisted, but his new building soon acquired its own mythology. Tales circulated, based largely on the accounts of Astor's employees and visitors who were bowled over by the lavish materials and decoration. It was said that 'there was no plot of ground in London on which so much money had been spent'. With a metal screen by Starkie Gardner costing £600 and the weathervane £120, the sums began to add up exponentially.[81]

Keen to show off the estate office when it reached completion, Astor organised a grand banquet for distinguished and noble guests. His guest list included an aristocratic roll call: Lord Iveagh, the Duchess of Buckingham and the Duchess of St Albans, among others. An after-dinner tour must have included an explanation of the literary programme he had initiated as well as the quality of the architecture. On this occasion, as Astor and the elderly Duchess of Cleveland ascended to the *piano nobile*, he prompted her by asking 'isn't [this] handsomer than any other staircase you ever saw', to which she replied that it was 'so much finer than our old staircase at Battle Abbey, which has been spoiled these two or three hundred years by the spurs of those stupid old knights!'[82] Astor also extended invitations to *The Pall Mall Gazette* for staff gatherings, and an afternoon tea party is recorded by Lord Ronald Sutherland Gower (1845–1916), author, art historian and sculptor. On this occasion, even this son of the Duke of Sutherland found himself 'quite oppressed with the crowd of duchesses that were there'. The connoisseur Gower gives some detailed commentary on the interiors and a wry assessment of 'Astor's new house, or rather palace, which I believe he calls his "office"… It is a most stately mansion, and looks for all the world as if one of the Elizabethan palaces which formerly lined the shores of the Thames had returned in redoubled splendour.'[83]

FIG. 93
'William Waldorf Astor, Englishman', chromolithograph by Albert Lavering, published in *Life* magazine, 11 May 1905 (private collection)

FIG. 94
Astor Estate Office, December 1895, photograph
by Bedford Lemere & Co. (reproduced by
permission of English Heritage, NMR)

Pride also induced Astor to commission the well-known architectural
photographic firm of Bedford Lemere and Company to record the building in
December 1895 (figs 19, 94). So new was it that Frith's sculptures were not
yet affixed to the outdoor stairs. The view of the portico facade appeared in *The
Architect* in November 1896 as a full-page illustration to announce the building
to a key audience. In 1898 the estate office appeared in a list of 'London's
Best Public Buildings' as 'perfect in its way', even though it was not public at
all.[84] Other accounts in the press focused on the high security at the estate office,
commenting it was 'nothing but a gigantic strong-room ... His office is probably
the most charming and best guarded building in the world, and deeds valued at
$100,000,000 are said to rest there.'[85] But not only money was contained within
– the owner himself had taken up almost permanent residence there. This became
common knowledge in 1905 when Astor, by then a British citizen, sought to

exercise his vote by virtue of being based at his Embankment address. The story hit the press once it was resolved, in his favour: 'Although Mr. Astor occasionally slept at Carlton House Terrace he usually resided at the offices on the Embankment.'[86] It seems he even tried to stop the London trams from running at night because the noise kept him awake. When the press got hold of this story, they had a field day: 'The Embankment must be kept quiet that he may sleep above his safes and strong rooms.'[87]

Frances Evelyn ('Daisy'), Countess of Warwick (1861–1938) recorded an anecdote of Astor at the estate office in her much later account, *Afterthoughts* (1931). When visiting Carlton House Terrace for a 'long and rather dull dinner', she made her departure, only for Astor to comment that he too was leaving: 'I do not sleep here since my wife died, but in the estate office on Victoria Embankment. There, at least, I am safe.' He invited her to call on him at his office, where she duly received his personal guided tour. Fascinated by the security, she noted that in the Great Room Astor pointed out one lever that, if pressed, could close every door in the house. Inside the strongroom he revealed bags filled with gold sovereigns: 'I keep ten thousand in cash in this room … You never know when you may want money.'[88] Departing, Lady Warwick felt she had woken from a dream that belonged more to the world of Wagner's *Nibelungenlied* than the present day. Her somewhat embroidered account, written thirty years after the event, may not present events exactly as they happened but it captures the spirit of Astor's cloistered life, alone amid his fairy-tale architectural interior and impenetrable strongrooms.

The estate office became Astor's true home where he withdrew from the world, even more so after a second tragic family death. In 1902 his daughter Gwendolyn, who had been nursed for many years by her sister Pauline, died of consumption, aged only thirteen. On the day of her death Astor announced the closure of the estate office, a rare occasion when his private feelings became public. His family life had its sorrows, but Pauline had stepped into her mother's shoes as hostess for her father. She would read aloud to Astor, probably in the Library at the estate office. He adored her and soon after her eighteenth birthday he commissioned the most fashionable portrait painter in London to portray her. Like Astor, John Singer Sargent was also an expatriate American. The gorgeous full-length, a homage to Van Dyck and Gainsborough, shows Pauline in fur-trimmed silk cape walking in an autumnal landscape (Royal Academy, 1899; private collection). This grand-manner portrait almost certainly hung at Carlton House Terrace where it could take centre stage at Astor's more formal entertainments. Pauline eventually made a happy marriage to Captain Herbert Spender-Clay, one of the richest commoners in Britain.

'Astor's new house, or rather palace, which I believe he calls his "office"'

Astor's formal demeanour and obsessively methodical behaviour served in some ways to protect him from emotional turmoil. Although there were rumours of another marriage (everyone was hinted at, from Lady Randolph Churchill to the Prince of Wales's daughter Princess Victoria), according to someone who knew him very well Astor was 'almost morbidly devoted to the memory of his wife'.[89] This sentiment rings true. His view of women stemmed from his early love, 'the princess of my fairy-tale', with his invariable attraction to the melancholy, lost, doomed heroines from literature and history, a theme that is laid bare in the decorative scheme. Around 1909, when about sixty, he did take a fancy to the mature Mrs (later Lady) Sackville-West (1862–1936), famous as the mother of Vita Sackville-West. They shared an *amitié amoureuse* for several years, and she visited him at Hever Castle and at his Italian villa in Sorrento.[90] But it seems unlikely that Astor did more than engage in dalliances with his aristocratic friends, still less that he brought them to the estate office for assignations, since he was always concerned with formal behaviour and proprieties.

Work filled in some of the gaps in Astor's life, but when he climbed his beloved Dumas-inspired staircase at the estate office and entered the Great Room and Library, he gained access to another world, satisfied that it had all been created to his exact specifications. Here Astor could lead the life he imagined in his dreams, encircled by a rich panoply of literary and historical characters to serve as his intimates; made of wood or stone, they were more reliable and reassuring than the living people who surrounded him. Perhaps only a fellow American expatriate, the writer Henry James, a contemporary of Astor's, could have drawn out his hidden and contradictory personality. Certainly, the complex relationship between an individual and their physical surroundings and possessions has its echoes in James's novel *The Spoils of Poynton* (1897).

At long last Astor received a title in 1916 when a barony was conferred on him in recognition of his financial contributions to a wide range of causes, from the Conservative party to the National Gallery (in 1904 he donated £5,000 towards the purchase of Titian's *Man with a Quilted Sleeve*). More relevant were his lavish benefactions to charities, such as the Red Cross and Order of St John, before and during the First World War. With his new title secured, he immediately commissioned a sculptural representation of his heraldic shield from William Silver Frith. This panel, with his coat of arms and supporters (Natty Bumppo and Uncas), was placed over the main entrance to the building (no longer in position). The following year Astor's further elevation to a viscountcy, as 1st Lord Astor of Hever Castle, necessitated an adjustment to the panel. It was important to him that there was a correct visual representation of his

The new estate office functioned as a means of embedding this wealthy American in English society and placing him on an equal footing with the old established families he so assiduously courted

ennoblement on the facade of the building. In the intervening years Astor's life had moved on considerably; he had acquired Hever Castle in Kent and devoted himself to remaking it. He bought *The Observer,* extending his newspaper empire, but by this time his sons were taking over the reins. In 1919, the year after he became Lord Astor of Hever Castle, he died aged seventy-one, having only enjoyed his title for two years.

When Astor commissioned the estate office in 1892, he had clear ideas for its practical requirements, yet he also understood that this building could enhance his position in society and, not least, express his own personal tastes. He was a very rich man, but in England he was an *arriviste;* money gave him a foothold in London, but alone it could not create an identity. The new estate office functioned as a means of embedding this wealthy American in English society and placing him on an equal footing with the old established families he so assiduously courted. His own, specifically American lineage is played out in some of the themes portrayed in the decoration. As in the country houses of the British aristocracy, family history is something to be celebrated. Astor created a miniature castle as a symbol of his family's position, yet this late-nineteenth-century architectural hybrid was at the same time a modern statement about commerce and business and the rock-solid reputation of Astor's property empire. The Tudor Gothic styling of the estate office clearly evoked the mansions of aristocratic dynasties with ancient lineage or, indeed, Oxbridge colleges. Inside, one might also imagine oneself in a comfortable London club, another familiar point of reference.

Astor took a leading role in the creation of the decorative scheme, derived from his favourite books, and relied on Pearson and his artistic team to execute it and refine the details. The years planning the design of his new estate office in the early 1890s were Astor's happiest as he looked to the future. Inside, the range of literary references and the perfection of the craftsmanship signalled his cultural awareness. Pearson and his team brought Astor's dreams of chivalric archetypes to life. The sheer intensity of the decoration throughout the building partakes of a *fin-de-siècle* mood in which fantasy merges with reality. The estate office became a stage on which Astor enacted a performance, as another American plutocrat, William Randolph Hearst, did several decades later at San Simeon in California or as the protagonist of cinema's *Citizen Kane* (1941) did at Xanadu. So compelling is the setting at Two Temple Place that we feel Astor's performance still reverberates there today.

THE ESTATE OFFICE
AFTER ASTOR

Once Astor died, his sons did not require the building so moved the operations of the Astor Estate to other premises. So particular and personal were the layout and design of the building to its original patron that it was difficult to find another use for it. Now dubbed Astor House, it was put up for sale in 1920. The sale catalogue is a revealing document that cannot disguise the fact that the building could never serve as a family home. With only one bedroom and several high-security strongrooms, it possessed a singular character that made it virtually unsaleable. For several years it stood empty, in a limbo state, with its strange stone gargoyles gazing out as the fog rolled in off the Thames, striking a sinister chord to those who passed by. Indeed, one writer, seizing on its remarkable cinematic qualities, thought 'it would make a nice little pied-a-terre in London for a movie king'.[91]

Publicity in 1920 brought the estate office to wider attention. *The Manchester Guardian* waxed lyrical about 'The Petit Palais of the Embankment'.[92] R. Randal Phillips's illustrated article in *Country Life* in September 1920 provided a rare chance to see inside the building with all Astor's possessions still in place (figs 88–90). Advertisements appeared in the press both in London and in the United States, where the *New York Times* noted that this 'roomy and artistic building' had been some time on the market.[93] At length, in 1922, a suitable solution came with its purchase by Sun Life Assurance Company of Canada, who renamed the building 'Sun of Canada House'. The largest insurance company in the country at this time, they wanted it as their headquarters and paid a rumoured sum of £80,000 for the freehold. This amount was far less than it had cost to build, but it was a solution for the Astor family (Astor's eldest son William had married the vivacious American divorcee Nancy Langhorne and she never did like her father-in-law's eccentric Anglo-American taste).

Sun Life initiated some new work and repairs, which Frank Pearson was on hand to supervise. J. Starkie Gardner created a new ornamental sign to hang outside the building. During this period in the 1920s the company waged a campaign with the London County Council to have the name of the road on which Astor

FIG. 95
Temple Place from the Embankment showing Electra House to the left and the Astor Estate Office (Incorporated Accountants' Hall) to the right, c.1937 (photograph: City of Westminster Archives Centre)

House stood changed from Approach Road, which they felt was unhelpful to those trying to find its offices. Eventually, they succeeded, with the new name, Temple Place, referring not only to neighbouring Middle Temple but also to the nearby London underground station. Only six years later, Astor House was put up for sale again as Sun Life had outgrown its premises. This time a quicker sale occurred in 1928 as the Society of Incorporated Accountants took on the freehold, which they held until 1959, renaming it Incorporated Accountants' Hall. Some fairly extensive internal modifications were carried out to make the premises a useful space for the Society. On the ground floor the subdivided main working area was partly cleared to become a library. In 1929 the Duke of York (and future King George VI), accompanied by the Duchess (later Queen Elizabeth, the Queen Mother), formally opened the building, an event recorded in newsreel footage and commemorated by a plaque in the entrance hall. Diligent custodians of these unique premises, the Society immediately commissioned an account of the building from J.R. Willis Alexander, which was published in 1928 (later editions, 1929, 1935).

THE WAR AND RECONSTRUCTION

The effects of World War II marked the next milestone in the history of Two Temple Place. In 1939 the roof and other parts of the building were protected with sandbags, the stained-glass windows went into storage,[94] and other fixtures and fittings were protected. The accountants relocated to temporary premises. The structure survived a parachute mine that fell in 1940 in Temple Gardens, devastating the Middle Temple Library next door. But in July 1944 an attack of German V1 flying bombs scored a direct hit on its western neighbour, Electra House (1929; figs 95–6), Herbert Baker's monolithic Head Office of Cable and Wireless Ltd, and that impact severely damaged the western side of the Incorporated Accountants' Hall: all its western stonework was injured beyond repair and one wing destroyed. This area had housed Astor's former bedroom with its strange gilded ceiling, which the Society used as their president's office. Worse was the flooding of the basement, prolonged by the stopcock's burial under debris; eventually, the flood was contained.[95] Later, during rebuilding, it was clear that the shock waves had played havoc with the structural alignment of walls, and internal woodwork also needed attention. Overhead, Starkie Gardner's weathervane was still in position; miraculously it escaped any damage.

Categorised by the War Damage Commission as 'partly demolished', the Incorporated Accountants' Hall required major rebuilding at the end of the war. This process took years to achieve. Initially, the Society consulted Sir Percy Thomas (1883–1969), a senior establishment figure (twice President of

Fig. 96
Electra House and Astor Estate Office (Incorporated Accountants' Hall) following bomb damage in July 1944 (photograph: City of Westminster Archives Centre)

the Royal Institute of British Architects), whose practice, the Percy Thomas Partnership, was based in Cardiff. In March 1949 work began on the restoration of the main structure. Builders Trollope and Colls had to take down 65 per cent of the outside wall to begin the reconstruction. The entire building was covered in scaffolding in order to reconstruct the roof, with new tiles put into position and the 'mellow salvaged tiles' being used on the front roof visible from the Embankment. Although it did not look radically different at the conclusion of the project, much had changed: the entrance portico was reconstructed with the addition of an oriel window above it (fig. 97); inside, above the vestibule, Astor's great strongroom was removed, and a new room was built in its place. In the Great Room much panelling was replaced or redone, one fireplace was removed and some of the carved Ivanhoe figures and heads in the frieze needed therapeutic attention. Severe damage to the Library meant creating a

FIG. 97
Two Temple Place showing
the new wing on the left

FIG. 98
Weathervane with Christopher
Columbus's ship, by J. Starkie Gardner

new simplified Tudor-style ceiling and erecting a new fireplace (Frith's original bizarre marble chimneypiece had been presented to Waldorf, the 2nd Viscount Astor, as it was so much a family heirloom). Throughout the reconstruction process Sir Percy Thomas ensured a high level of craftsmanship. Where new work had to be done it was invariably of an excellent standard; recovering original work was equally painstaking, with areas such as the Cosmatesque stone floor in the staircase hall repaired and ground to a new finish. Some scars were left on the ebony columns as a badge of what the building had gone through. Amazingly, the Shakespeare frieze by Nicholls was completely unharmed.[96]

In celebratory spirit, in August 1950 the newspaper picture agencies photographed Starkie Gardner's gilded Columbus weathervane as it was repositioned on the top of the building (fig. 99, p. 96). Fully completed in 1951 at a cost of £96,000,[97] the building reopened. A handsome stone plaque was set into the wall of the entrance hall, inconspicuously positioned, proclaiming: 'Erected 1895. Architect J.L. Pearson, R.A. Reconstructed 1951 after Enemy Action. Architect Sir Percy Thomas, P.P.R.I.B.A.' In the 1950s the architectural merits of Two Temple Place were endorsed when Nikolaus Pevsner included it in *The Buildings of England* (1957). Shortly after, it attained Grade II*-listed building status.

The Society of Accountants remained in their palace on the Embankment until 1959, when they sold it for £168,000. In 1960 the healthcare conglomerate Smith & Nephew Associated Companies Limited, inventors of 'Elastoplast', moved into their new headquarters which they named Two Temple Place. They proved to be equally good guardians, undertaking the heavy structural work of constructing a reinforced concrete raft with piles extending 90 feet (27.4 metres) below into the London clay.[98] Some internal remodelling also occurred, with Percy Thomas overseeing a new extension, and this office wing (extending beyond the footprint of the original wing with Astor's bedroom, which had itself been completely reconstructed after the War) reached completion in 1967. The decision was taken that the style of this new build should harmonise with the original structure, and so craftsmen and designers who could match the vigorous carving of Nathaniel Hitch were recruited. Today this section appears as a convincing addition to Pearson's original.[99] During this era Smith & Nephew's Chairman, Mr G.E. Leavey, took a particular interest in the history of the building and prepared a short publication, which came out in 1971. He approached that great proponent of Victorian architecture, Sir John Betjeman, who willingly contributed a brief foreword to the booklet.

BETJEMAN AND PEARSON

A great enthusiast of Pearson's work, Betjeman wrote in glowing terms about it long before anyone valued high Victorian architecture. He relished the way that the architect's churches all had 'thrillingly romantic' outlines, with noble spires rising into the sky, and how the tall, narrow, vaulted interiors created dramatic vistas. He wrote of Pearson's St Stephen's, Bournemouth: 'It is worth travelling 200 miles and being sick in a coach to have seen the inside of this many-vistaed church.'[100] Betjeman appreciated Pearson's scholarly medievalism, with its admixture of French Gothic, which produced an 'Early English of his own'. Most of all he seems to have admired how the architect's deep religious beliefs informed his work. These effects were all for the glory of God; at Two Temple Place Pearson's dramatic treatment was for the glory of Astor.

Betjeman jumped at the chance to assess Two Temple Place, which he considered 'one of the most attractive private houses in London'. His introduction to the booklet of 1971 has not as yet been included in collections of this writer's known prose works, so is a genuine rediscovery. With his searching eye, he understood that one of the key features of Pearson's work was 'his delight in simple planning and letting the materials be their own decoration'. Throughout the building Pearson allowed the natural materials to speak for themselves: exotic woods, rare marble, coloured stone, all these create an environment of great beauty or, in Betjeman's phrase, 'a little masterpiece'. The author's letter to Smith & Nephew's chairman expresses his appreciation of the care the company was taking to ensure that the rooms in the new extension on the western side of the building harmonised with the original design. They avoided a trend Betjeman deplored of demolishing and putting up a slab.[101] Once the booklet came out, he wrote to the chairman from his flat in Cloth Fair in the City in typically playful spirit, providing the company with a jaunty testimonial: 'God bless Smith & his Nephew & all their products. They have lightened the dull December of the days of their obliged servant John Betjeman who here drinks to them all and to John Loughborough Pearson, his son Frank and Sir Percy Thomas.' Far from being a myopic Victorian, Betjeman, the realistic historian, assessed Two Temple Place as a collaboration and a 'triple triumph' of all three generations of architects, with the additions and revision partaking of the same spirit as the original. It was a rare coup to get the eminent writer to comment on the building, and his observations still add to our understanding of it today.

These effects were all for the glory of God; at Two Temple Place Pearson's dramatic treatment was for the glory of Astor

TWO TEMPLE PLACE IN THE TWENTY-FIRST CENTURY

In 1999 Two Temple Place changed hands for only the fourth time since it left the Astor family. Having immediately recognised the cultural significance of the building, Richard Q. Hoare made the visionary purchase of Two Temple Place for the charitable trust he had founded in 1983, in order to safeguard the house's future. The Bulldog Trust has devoted as much attention to this unique amalgam of art and architecture as its predecessors. Today it is not only the charity's home but also serves as an increasingly busy centre for its charitable and cultural activities. It is regularly open to the public, with annual special exhibitions showcasing museum collections outside the metropolis as well as frequent charitable events and tours coordinating with private hire. Thanks to these efforts, Pearson's building is better known than it has ever been, with its grand reopening in 2011 prompting much enthusiastic assessment.[102] At long last in the twenty-first century this 'little masterpiece' has progressed far beyond its role as the sanctuary of the wealthy William Waldorf Astor to take its place as one of the gems of later Victorian art, architecture and design.

NOTES

[1] In 1971 John Betjeman wrote a foreword to a short brochure about Two Temple Place produced by the Smith & Nephew Group, the occupants of the building from 1960 to 1999.

[2] The section on Pearson's building has been expanded by Simon Bradley in the most recent edition of *The Buildings of England: London 6. Westminster*, London 2003.

[3] 'The Late Mr Pearson, R.A.', *The Times,* 13 December 1897, p. 8.

[4] Pearson's work has been well studied by Anthony Quiney in his book, *John Loughborough Pearson*, New Haven and London 1979, and in several articles since then. He has informed me that 'the Pearson archive of office papers was sent for scrap at the beginning of the Second World War'. A granddaughter saved a few items, and some drawings went to the RIBA (private communication, 24 July 2012). See Jill Lever (ed.), *Catalogue of the Drawings Collection of the Royal Institute of British Architects: O–R*, Farnborough 1976, p. 41, which includes twenty Pearson drawings.

[5] *The Times*, 20 October 1919, p. 16.

[6] The history of the Astor dynasty both before and after William Waldorf Astor is well covered in such sources as Michael Astor, *Tribal Feeling*, London 1963; Gavin Astor, *The Astor Family*, London 1970; Virginia Cowles, *The Astors: The Story of a Transatlantic Family*, London 1979; David Sinclair, *Dynasty: The Astors and their Times*, London 1983; Derek Wilson, *The Astors 1793–1992: Landscape with Millionaires*, London 1993; Axel Madsen, *John Jacob Astor: America's First Multimillionaire,* New York 2001; and Julius Kaplan, *When the Astors Owned New York,* New York 2007; for a more specialised study, see Richard Kenin, *Return to Albion: Americans in England 1760–1940*, Washington, D.C., 1979.

[7] William Waldorf Astor, *Silhouettes, 1855–1885,* London 1917, p. 75.

[8] As a result of his election, he was entitled to call himself 'the Honorable' William Waldorf Astor. He did not receive his British titles until many years later.

[9] Astor, *Silhouettes*, p. 58.

[10] Eventually, he formed an important collection, which he displayed at Cliveden in Buckinghamshire (where significant pieces can still be seen) and later at Hever Castle. Regarding the former, see Antonia Boström, 'A Bronze Group of the Rape of Proserpina at Cliveden House in Buckinghamshire', *Burlington Magazine*, CXXXII (1990), pp. 829–40.

[11] *Morning Post*, 17 February 1886, p. 2.

[12] *Pall Mall Gazette*, 11 November 1890, p. 6.

[13] 'Our London Letter', *Dundee Courier and Argus*, 21 July 1892. (Here and in some of the following citations of periodical and newspaper articles, sourced via internet listings, page numbers are only occasionally given. Although these papers may have been local in both the UK and the USA, they picked up stories from national and international news agencies.)

[14] *Leeds Mercury*, 19 August 1893.

[15] J.R. Willis Alexander, *Incorporated Accountants' Hall: Its History and Architecture,* 3rd edn, London 1935, p. 6, cites a view of Temple Gardens published in 1861 that shows Gwynne's as a big open-roofed warehouse, which may be the same as or similar to the engraving in the *Illustrated London News*, 9 November 1861.

[16] The newspaper's offices were on Northumberland Street, and later the Pall Mall publications were at 18 Charing Cross Road (until about 1904).

[17] The confined nature of the site is visible in a photograph of the School Board Offices taken by Bedford Lemere in April 1894. Astor's plot can be seen to the west filled with low shacks, which probably represent work in progress on the Astor Estate Office. The photograph is reproduced in Nicholas Cooper, *The Photography of Bedford Lemere & Co.,* Swindon 2011, p. 74.

[18] *The Times,* 13 December 1897, p. 8 ('The Late Mr Pearson, R.A.').

[19] Ibid.

[20] The brother of Jemima Christian (1829–65) was an architect, as was her cousin, Ewan Christian (1814–95), who had a long and eminent career, culminating in the building of the National Portrait Gallery in London.

[21] Clive Aslet, 'The first Astor at Hever Castle', *Art at Auction: The Year at Sotheby's 1981–1982,* London 1982, pp. 10–15.

[22] Cosmo Monkhouse, 'The Late John Loughborough Pearson, R.A.', *Pall Mall Magazine,* XV (1898), p. 110.

[23] By the early 1940s some of Pearson's antiquarian books had been donated to the RIBA by his son, for example Augustus Welby Pugin, *Ornaments of the XVth and XVIth Centuries*, London c.1845, and J.D. Harding, *Gothic Ornaments, Selected from Various Ancient Buildings,* London 1840.

[24] *Particulars of The Astor Estate Office, Victoria Embankment, W.C.,* sale catalogue. It seems likely that John Coode Adams, Astor's solicitor and business manager, whose firm was arranging the sale, provided the details in this catalogue. My thanks to Roger Bettridge, County Archivist, and Sally Mason, Archivist, at the Centre for Buckinghamshire Studies for their help.

[25] *Ellensburgh Localizer,* 6 May 1893, p. 2.

[26] *Lewiston Evening Journal,* 20 October 1919.

[27] His assistant John E. Newberry wrote of this treatment in 'The Work of John L. Pearson, R.A. Part II: Domestic', *Architectural Review,* I (1896–7), p. 80.

[28] The view from the entrance portico showed the plain brick side of the extended London School Board Offices, so Pearson erected a stone wall covering it up. This wall, subdivided with piers and panels, had diverting decorations in the form of gargoyle heads (although one writer mentions vases).

[29] The family firm established earlier in the nineteenth century was run at this time by John Thompson junior (d. 1898). I am grateful to Richard Hunt, archivist at Peterborough Culture and Leisure, for information that clarified Thompson's work at the Astor Estate Office.

[30] Frank Pearson to Lionel Wood, 8 October 1923 (when the mechanism needed replacing), letter in the Bulldog Trust Archive.

[31] *Journal of the Royal Institute of British Architects,* October 1952, p. 439.

[32] *Washington Times,* 22 October 1905, 'Castle of Commerce …'.

[33] *Journal of the Royal Institute of British Architects,* V, no. 5 (January 1898), p. 113.

[34] Harriet Richardson and Colin Thom, 'The Work of the Pearsons at Middlesex Hospital Chapel: a decorative *tour de force*, *Apollo,* CXLV (1997), pp. 11–18. For the chapel project, unlike for the Astor Estate Office, a series of letters from Pearson survives, and as Richardson and Thom explain, he had an exceptionally high level of involvement in all aspects of the building and decoration. His concern with all details, particularly of decoration, would certainly have been the same for a prestige project such as the commission from Astor for the estate office.

[35] See 'Nathaniel Hitch: Architectural Sculptor and Modeller', *Occasional Monograph,* no. 1, February 2010, Truro Cathedral, Truro.

[36] Hitch was also heavily involved in the Pearsons' work at Cliveden for Astor.

[37] Hitch probably came to Pearson's attention through Thomas Nicholls, who modelled decorative figures for William Burges's Cardiff Castle from the 1870s onwards. Hitch worked under Nicholls as one of the executant carvers who travelled down to Cardiff to sculpt on site (J. Mordaunt Crook, *William Burges and the High Victorian Dream*, Chicago and London 1981, p. 402 n. 5).

[38] Albums of Hitch's work in the Archive of the Henry Moore Institute, Leeds, show these elaborate urns.

[39] Hitch's sense of the grotesque is also evident in his decoration for the Black Friar Public House (after 1905) near Blackfriars Bridge: see Philip Ward-Jackson, *Public Sculpture of the City of London*, Public Sculpture of Britain, vol. VII, Liverpool 2003, pp. 310ff.

[40] Starkie Gardner's book, *Ironwork: From the Earliest Times to the End of the Mediaeval Period,* was published in 1893; he was also working on books about English enamels and further studies on English ironwork, which came out in the late 1890s. He later attracted royal attention when King Edward VII visited his forge, prompting him to bill himself 'Metalworker to the King', which seems to have been an informal title.

[41] Although early writers call this ship a caravel, it is a larger type known as a carrack. The other two ships, the *Nina* and the *Pinta*, were small caravels.

[42] Despite his surname, he was not related to the well-known Victorian painter, William Powell Frith.

His father Henry Frith, also a carver, worked in various counties, settling in Leicestershire and eventually moving to Gloucestershire. On the Friths father and son, see the website, *Mapping the Practice and Profession of Sculpture in Britain,* Glasgow University, http://sculpture.gla.ac.uk/

[43] For Webb he executed architectural sculpture at the Metropolitan Life Assurance Building (1892–3) on Moorgate and, after 1905, on the exterior of the Victoria and Albert Museum, where he contributed the figures of John Bacon the Elder and Grinling Gibbons on the Cromwell Road facade, as well as other elements of architectural carving, including the royal arms above the main entrance.

[44] W.S. Frith, 'Wood-carving and wood-carvers', *Journal of the Royal Institute of British Architects,* III, no. 3 (1896), p. 217.

[45] When the building housed private companies and was not open to the public, these lamps could at least be seen by most and, as a result, they have received full appreciation as masterworks of later Victorian sculpture; see Susan Beattie, *The New Sculpture*, New Haven and London, 1983, p. 124.

[46] I am very grateful to John Liffen, Curator of Communications, Science Museum, who helped to identify the objects in each sculpture and provided useful background information. Also at the Science Museum Ian Blatchford and Tilly Blyth kindly facilitated my enquiries.

[47] The theme of electricity in the decoration of the Astor Estate Office was in advance of the construction in 1929 of its next-door neighbour, Herbert Baker's Electra House, the headquarters of Cable and Wireless Ltd.

[48] There are no historic photographs of this room, but the plan clearly shows how it was used.

[49] The fate of the Starkie Gardner grille is not known, but its appearance can be seen in one of the unpublished photographs taken by *Country Life* for an article on the building in 1920 (see n. 57).

[50] The name, derived from the Cosmatus family of marble workers (active second half of the thirteenth century), became the generic one for paved floors of this type.

[51] Quiney, *Pearson,* p. 115 and ill. p. 117.

[52] J.R. Willis Alexander, *Incorporated Accountants' Hall: Its History and Architecture,* London 1928, p. 7. Davison probably supervised Italian craftsmen to lay the marble, as he had done for Pearson at the Middlesex Hospital Chapel in the early 1890s (see n. 34).

[53] *The Cornish See & Cathedral: Historical and Architectural Notes,* Truro 1888, p. 17.

[54] William Barrow's translation, which was published in London in 1846, is still in print and widely used.

[55] Alexander, *Incorporated Accountants' Hall* (1928), p. 7.

[56] This coat of arms was created when Astor was raised to a viscountcy in 1917. A sculpted version appeared over the doorway to the house.

[57] R. Randal Phillips, 'The Astor Estate Office on Victoria Embankment', *Country Life,* 25 September 1920, p. 403.

[58] Alexander, *Incorporated Accountants' Hall* (1928), p. 7.

[59] The other chimneypiece differed in that it was designed to contain a painting – a portrait of William Waldorf Astor's great-grandfather. The original arrangement can be seen in fig. 83.

[60] A reduced statuette version of the figure of Florence Nightingale from Arthur G. Walker's memorial to her (1915) in Waterloo Place, London, which was probably added during the Smith & Nephew era at Temple Place.

[61] According to one source, the chandeliers were executed by Starkie Gardner but this has yet to be verified.

[62] *Architectural Review,* I (1897), p.77.

[63] George Frampton, 'On Colouring Sculpture', *Studio, 3* (1894), p. 79, although the article is about plaster reliefs, the same principal could be applied to metal work.

[64] Quiney tells this story based on Frank's daughter's recollections: Quiney, *Pearson,* p. 174.

[65] On La Farge's work for Vanderbilt's mansion c.1880, see Wayne Craven, *Gilded Mansions: Grand Architecture and High Society,* New York 2009, pp. 101ff. Tiffany was also producing some landscape designs in stained glass that were incorporated into interior schemes.

[66] Megan Aldrich (ed.), *The Craces: Royal Decorators, 1768–1899*, London 1990, pp. 128–32.

[67] Quoted in John William Robertson-Scott, *The Life and Death of a Newspaper,* London 1952, p. 378.

[68] The portraits by Baker, Madrazo and Herkomer from the family's collection are now at Cliveden, Buckinghamshire, in the care of the National Trust.

[69] A sale of the remains of this collection took place at Sotheby's, London, on 21 June 1988.

[70] Alexander, *Incorporated Accountants' Hall* (1928), p. 13, mentions a joiner named Moos who participated in the project. This seems to be an error for Moss, a wood-working firm in Paddington that made the fireplace in the Great Room and must have done most related work, such as the flooring throughout the building.

[71] The fireplace and chimneypiece were taken to Cliveden; recently, it has been dismantled and placed in storage.

[72] Astor, *Silhouettes,* pp. 74–5.

[73] 14 September 1896 (private collection); an attached note indicates that copies were lodged with Pauline, Astor's daughter, and his manager, John Coode Adams.

[74] In fact he said that it was the 'newspapers that make the country unfit for a gentleman to live in', although this is often cited as an example of his dislike of America as a whole.

[75] *Manchester Guardian,* 5 January 1900, p. 6.

[76] *Life,* XLV (11 May 1905).

[77] *Daily Mail and Empire,* 8 February 1899.

[78] 'London Letter', *Yorkshire Herald,* 20 November 1895, p. 4.

[79] *St James Weekly News,* 6 April 1895 (a story picked up the next day by the *Baltimore American*).

[80] 'Astor's London Office', *The New York World,* reprinted in the *Youngstown Vindicator,* 13 April 1896.

[81] Robertson-Scott, *Life and Death,* p. 304.

[82] This often repeated anecdote derived from the London paper, *Tit-Bits,* and appeared in many sources around the world, including the *Daily Argus,* 15 April 1899, p. 6.

[83] Lord Ronald Sutherland Gower, *Old Diaries: 1881–1901,* London 1902, p. 298.

[84] *Morning Record,* 25 April 1898.

[85] Original story in the *Daily Mail,* reprinted as far afield as New Zealand in the *Auckland Star,* 24 September 1900.

[86] An article in the *Washington Times* (22 October 1905) explained Astor's position to an American audience: he was entitled to a vote in each area where he owned property; the story also appeared in the *Manchester Guardian,* 13 September 1905.

[87] *Manufacturers' and Farmers' Journal,* 12 October 1905.

[88] Frances, Countess of Warwick, *Afterthoughts,* London 1931, p. 114.

[89] *Eastern Free Press,* 15 January 1907, regarding 'a dispatch from London'.

[90] Victoria Glendinning, *Vita: The Life of Vita Sackville-West,* London 1983, pp. 32, 60.

[91] *Manchester Guardian,* 28 August 1920.

[92] Ibid.

[93] *New York Times,* 2 October 1921, p. 107.

[94] *The Accountant,* 5 September 1959, p. 156.

[95] *The West End at War:* www.westendatwar.org.uk/page_id__204_path__0p28p.aspx

[96] Much of the information in the previous paragraph comes from 'Reconstruction of the Incorporated Accountants' Hall, Victoria Embankment, E.C.1 [*sic*]', *Journal of the Royal Institute of British Architects,* October 1952, pp. 439–41.

[97] *The Times,* 23 May 1951, p. 8.

[98] *2 Temple Place: Headquarters of the Smith & Nephew Group,* London [1971].

[99] In 1984 the reception area was remodelled again.

[100] John Betjeman, *First and Last Loves: Essays on Towns and Architecture,* London 1952, p. 13.

[101] John Betjeman, foreword, *2 Temple Place,* unpaged.

[102] Foremost amongst these responses is Michael Hall's excellent article, 'A Palace for a Plutocrat', *Country Life,* 4 January 2012, pp. 38–43.